THE GREENWICH
A COMPANION TO THE HOME OF GMT

Published by
Librario Publishing Ltd

ISBN: 1-904440-28-2

Copies can be ordered via the Internet
www.librario.com

or from:

Brough House, Milton Brodie, Kinloss
Moray IV36 2UA
Tel /Fax No 00 44 (0)1343 850 617

Printed and bound by Antony Rowe Ltd, Eastbourne

© 2003 Margaret Kaye
This book or any part of it may not be
reproduced without permission from the author

The Greenwich Effect

A Companion To The Home Of GMT

Margaret Kaye

Librario

CONTENTS

DEDICATION		7
ACKNOWLEDGEMENTS		8
INTRODUCTION		10

PART ONE

1. The UNESCO World Heritage Site Greenwich — 13
   A Short Briefing and Bird's Eye View as the Crow Flies
2. *The Cutty Sark* — 33
3. The Painted Hall and Chapel — 41
   Old Royal Naval College and Seamen's Hospital
4. The National Maritime Museum — 50
5. Time Out in the Park with Captain Cook — 63
6. The Queen's House — 69
7. Time Out on One Tree Hill with the Tudors — 78
8. The Royal Observatory Greenwich:
   - i   How and When – Now and Then — 85
   - ii Prime Meridian of the World at 0.00 Degrees Longitude — 90
   - iii Flamsteed House:
     A) Home and Workplace of the First Royal Astronomer — 93
     B) Galleries of Time and John Harrison's Very Notable Watch — 98
   - iv The Home of Time Rose Garden — 105
   - v   Meridian Building and Planetarium – Telescopes in Transit — 110

PART TWO: *ZOOMING INTO HISTORY*

1. **Telling Times: Sundials to Caesium Atoms**   123
2. **Creating the Compass**   130
3. **Roger Bacon** – Magnifying Glass   132
4. **Galileo** – Testing Times for Pendulums and Popes   137
5. **All At Sea Without Longitude**   140
6. **John Harrison** – the Trials and Triumphs Clocking Time at Sea   144
7. **Michael Faraday** – Electrifying Magnetism   151
8. **Currents and Cables**   161
9. **Isaac Newton and Albert Einstein** – Reason and Relativity in the Heavens of William Herschel and Edwin Hubble   167
10. **TV Times** – Monitors and Computers with Chips   177

FINALE:

A) John 'Longitude' Harrison – Life at Barrow upon Humber **180**

B) John Flamsteed, first Royal Astronomer – A Living at Burstow and boyhood in Derby   **191**

TIPS FOR TOURISTS and MAP   197

APPENDICES

    A few Parishioners of Greenwich and visitor Peter the Great   217
    Downriver to the Thames Barrier   221
    Upriver to *HMS Belfast*   223
    The Golden Hinde   225
    Shakespeare's Globe Theatre   227

USEFUL ADDRESSES   230
NOTABLE DATES   231
BIBLIOGRAPHY   241

John Flamsteed, 1646-1719
First Astronomer Royal

This book is dedicated with respect and humility to all who made the achievements of Greenwich available to Mankind, Then and Now

Front Cover:
Top left – The time ball at the Royal Observatory, Greenwich (ROG)
Top centre – The famous timepiece 'H4' (ROG)
Top right – John 'Longitude' Harrison
Bottom left – The 24-hour Shepherd Clock outside the ROG
Bottom right – Stern of the Cutty Sark in dry dock, Greenwich

ACKNOWLEDGEMENTS

My grateful thanks are due to the following for permitting access to reference material, facilities to view and personal interview in the preparation of this book:–

Director of Friends National Maritime Museum Ms Polly Larner and Head of the Royal Observatory Dr Gloria Clifton for kindly reading the relevant sections of the final manuscript. Also Mr David Taylor of the Picture Library and the Staff of the Caird Library NMM for their cooperation.

The office of the County Archivist, Surrey History Centre, Woking, and Dr M O'Sullivan, County and Diocesan Archivist, Derbyshire Record Office; The Public Records Office, Kew, for allowing publication of the text of Charles II's Royal Warrants for the appointment of the First Royal Astronomer.

The Vicar of Holy Trinity Church at Barrow upon Humber, The Reverend John Girtchen; Churchwarden John Cherry; Verger Mrs Marjorie North and Mr James North; Post Mistress Mrs Carol Clark; Head Teacher Peter Croton and the Secretary of the John Harrison Church of England Primary School. Mr John Amos who loaned me a copies of 'John Harrison's Village' (researched and compiled by Nick Lyons and fellow members of the local branch of the WEA, Barrow upon Humber) and 'The Manor of Barrow' written by Helen Gray (Martin) & Neil Wilkyn. Also Christine Bloor, current secretary of Barrow upon Humber WEA; Ken Heath and Kees van den Bos who have willingly supplied photographs and prints. The Earl of Yarborough who gave permission for me to view John Harrison's Turret Clock; Mr Harry Johnson who made my visit to Brocklesby Park so informative and happily supplied extra photographs; Mr

Henry Rayment of the Estate Office, and the staff at Cleethorpes Tourist Information Office who pointed me in the right direction.

Churchwarden Ann Sheppard of St Bartholomew's Church, Burstow, Surrey, for village history and photographs and the hardworking parishioners who eagerly welcomed me into John Flamsteed's church in the midst of preparing for their harvest festival; the staff and customer at Smallfield Post Office who made sure I reached Burstow safely, and Win Clavering and all the staff at Woolsthorpe Manor, Lincolnshire, who courteously allowed me to photograph and made my visit otherwise so enjoyable. Thanks also to Leslie and staff at the Tourist Information Centre, Assembly Rooms, Derby, and Richard and Edward Felix at the Derby Heritage Centre, Old Tudor Hall.

Finally, my heartfelt thanks to publisher Mark Lawson of Librario, Elgin, for his unstinting support and acumen in bringing this project to fruition; his assistant Kay; Tommy Smith for his expert editing and advice; Stephen Young for his patience and technical skills in producing the final result, and Zoë for her artistry and design of the cover.

INTRODUCTION

'What's the time?' is probably the most frequent and essential question ever asked – with 'What's to eat?' a close second! Consciously or unconsciously, Greenwich Mean Time is an everyday, global fact of life. Our clocks and watches are programmed by it for accurate measurement whatever our time zone; we glance at each of them often and unhesitatingly, for sheer necessity. We listen, too, for familiar pips and chimes. Our computer age and atomic clocks are derived from, and dependent, on it. Providing the immediate answer for the time of day and night has not always been as easy as modern technology now permits.

Those of you who come to see for yourselves the role that Greenwich has played in encouraging and collating man's knowledge of navigation and time-measurement skills throughout the ages could perhaps feel a little overwhelmed by all there is on-site to absorb and enjoy; especially if you have available only a few hours in one short day of this universe, and perhaps not the opportunity to indulge in all the excellent literature available on these topics.

Some people may not have visited yet. Distance and infirmity may make the idea impossible for others. Those who came once as children may still cherish happy and exciting memories of a school excursion or holiday treat. Some may be thinking about coming, to see what all the fuss is about.

Commuters and others travelling by road through the majestic complex of buildings where the domes of the Royal Observatory encompass, from the horizon, the National Maritime Museum in Greenwich Park below, may perhaps mentally register to take a look inside again but somehow never quite get round to doing so.

Some of us, I suspect, may have considerable affinity with Charles Lamb who would write in 1815: "Nothing puzzles me more than time and space; yet nothing troubles me less, as I never think about them".

Today, we have very advanced technology to help aid our understanding.

For anyone interested in Greenwich and Mean Time this journal has been compiled – by a layman for laymen – and intended simply to provide enough knowledge to aid your enjoyment of the genius and the glory of this recently designated UNESCO World Heritage Site where uniquely 'time stands still', whether you are armchair traveller or on-site with guidebook.

For simplicity the main text is divided into Parts One and Two, complimented by the Tips for Tourists section. Part One focuses on the numerous attractions and what to look out for – with some background information for good measure. The Tips for Tourists section is indexed A-Z for easy reference and provides information on ways of travelling to Greenwich, times of access and general information. A map shows the location of convenient bus stops and the local railway stations.

Part Two delves deeper into history and briefly outlines the breakthroughs in scientific knowledge that made a profound contribution on the effect of Greenwich Mean Time, as it became irrevocably established in the centre of the canvas of man's achievements and around which we are forever weaving. The Notable Dates section is designed for dipping into and endeavours to include some of the many other happenings in the world before, during and after the 'goings-on' at the 'green place with harbour' which afforded such a milestone for mankind.

On a few occasions I have included two abbreviations. NMM stands for the National Maritime Museum and ROG for the Royal Observatory Greenwich. As we will discover, to see one without the other is unthinkable. Access is now free to all buildings. Admission charges remain at present for the *Cutty Sark* which is endeavouring to fund major restoration and for special exhibitions. However, donations are always welcome!

At the time of going to press, the Nelson, Sea Power and Cargoes Galleries are temporarily closed for essential repairs and the preparations for the major exhibition marking the 400th anniversary of the death of Queen Elizabeth I to be held from 1 May to 14 September 2003.

The only problem may be finding time for all these attractions – and no pun is intended!

Margaret Kaye
March 2003

THE UNESCO WORLD HERITAGE SITE GREENWICH

A Short Briefing and Bird's Eye View as The Crow Flies

Whatever your mode of transport to this small area of approximately one square mile (2.5 Sq Km), snugly ensconced from north to south between Blackheath and the River Thames just six miles (10 Km) downriver from London, you are in a place that is no stranger to visitors.

Naturally the Romans came, displaced the Celts and obligingly built a road through Kent direct from the coast at Dover, via Canterbury and Rochester. Easily able to park their chariots, the legions ferried up the marshy flatlands to Londinium and constructed the first known bridge across the River Thames on the sandbanks at Southwark, in AD 60. A thousand years later, the Danes rowed their formidably-prowed long boats up the Thames Estuary, bringing with them in 1012 the abducted 29th Archbishop of Canterbury, Alfege. A stretch of Watlynge Strete, the Old English name for so much of the Roman's extensive road system, survives as nearby Shooter's Hill. In 1859, Charles Dickens vividly began his harrowing account of *A Tale of Two Cities* on it; he wrote also of the area in other novels.

The saga of Greenwich, however, can be found quite simply beside Greenwich Pier in the World Heritage Site Visitor Information Centre, splendidly and conveniently housed in the Pepys Building; the ornate exterior decorated with busts denoting the naval supremacy of bygone years. Today, alongside, the masts and rigging of the preserved 'Queen of Clippers', the *Cutty Sark*, tower overhead from her small dry dock.

On entering the Visitor Centre, you are walking into the former fives and racquets courts built during the Victorian era and used by the Old Royal Naval College. Later accorded a roof, the space was utilised as a mechanical laboratory. Now, as a Visitor Information Centre, the building provides an easy-to-follow and graphic account of Greenwich's history and famous achievements. There is also a shop, cloakrooms and the Tiltyard Café, named in recognition of the days of the turbulent Tudor dynasty that so greatly patronised and enriched the area. The adjacent Tourist Information Centre also has much on offer and will give you a free map.

Already you may feel familiar with some of the surroundings. If you arrived by train at the mainline station – the world's first suburban line opened in 1838 – you may have walked to the Visitor Centre passing en route to your right the cottages and neat gardens of the Queen Elizabeth's College Almshouses. Within a few minutes the rust-brown brick facade of the slender Meridian Clocktower, with its distinctive blue and white dial, denoting the former Town Hall built in the 1930s adjacent to the local library comes into view; the observation platform at the top is unfortunately not open to public viewing.

The heart of the bustling and small town centre is soon reached and the imposing shabby-grey exterior of Nicholas Hawksmoor's parish church shows us where Archbishop Alfege was martyred, for refusing to allow a ransom to be paid to the disobliging Danes. He had good reason, for they had already double-crossed him and the poor citizens of Canterbury. Only one main road runs through the town centre, designed in the 1830s by Joseph Kay. Environmental and scientific considerations did not allow the railway to extend above ground across Greenwich Park, originally enclosed as a royal hunting ground in the 15th century. The royal palaces were built fronting the river.

Paradoxically, the distances are small between the places of interest in a place so universally renowned for calculating measurements of time and space on a grand scale. It is just a few minutes walk along Greenwich Church Street to the Cutty Sark Gardens, built on the site of the narrow alleys and crowded dwellings which served the ancient fishing port for centuries. The surface areas of some of those tiny living spaces are now marked out on the ground beneath your feet.

Nearby is the illustriously-named Cutty Sark for Maritime Greenwich Station of the Docklands Light Railway, only a few minutes from the Visitor Centre.

Maybe, like the Danes, you came by river. Unlike them, however, comfortably aboard a pleasure cruiser and entertained with a commentary of the famous, and infamous, landmarks. Beyond the Tower of London, passing through the on-going regeneration of the once blitz-ridden East London, the roll call of the evocative names of the old docklands refers now mainly to marinas and luxury dwellings. For despite some post-war survival, the London Docks were finally rendered obsolete during the 1970s. The sophisticated navigational techniques pioneered during the war years led to the computerisation of loading systems. The use of containers, commercially developed from the design of the roll-on/roll-off Normandy invasion landing craft in 1944, needed the accommodating deeper waters of coastal ports. Advanced technology would also take over on land. The Docklands Light Railway was built during the 1980s and also provides a very scenic route to reach Greenwich; fleeting and fascinating views are available if you travelled this way from the City or Tower Gateway. A few stops out brings you to Limehouse or old 'Chinatown'. Once known as a hive of industry for kilns and home to generations of seafarers, it remains presided over by the majestic, early 18th century St Anne's Church, also masterminded by Nicholas Hawksmoor, one-time clerk to Christopher Wren.

The Limehouse Basin is clearly visible as a smart marina full of gleaming small craft. Built in 1820, it now serves a very different function from its original purpose; that of loading cargoes onto the narrow canal boats for nationwide distribution on the newly dug canal system. Close-up, Britain's tallest building looms over Canada Square, the Canary Wharf Tower at 800 ft high (244 metres). Completed in 1990, clustering cranes and massive construction gear remain busily interspersed with the up-market business and social amenities at ground level. Afar, golden fish float incongruously on the horizon above the 1000-year-old Billingsgate Market that moved to the Isle of Dogs in 1982 from London Bridge; the oldest market in London and specializing in fish since the 16th century. Then, the unmistakeable 'maritime-masts' of the more recent and controversial Millennium Dome. Covering an area the size of Trafalgar Square and as high as Nelson's Column on Greenwich Peninsula, the Millennium Dome is just 800 metres (half a mile) downstream from the Visitor Centre.

If you want to see Greenwich from across the river, there is no need to be on a boat. You can do as the Venetian painter Canaletto did and view from Island Gardens, opposite the Visitor Centre, on the northern bank of the Thames on the Isle of Dogs.

The Docklands Light Railway has a station at Island Gardens. If you came otherwise, it is swift and simple to travel one stop to Island Gardens from the Cutty Sark for Maritime Greenwich Station. Opposite the ticket office in this station is a brightly painted half-section of the several-metres-in-diameter boring machine faceplate, dubbed by some as 'Dolores', that burrowed and drilled under the Thames to construct the rail track from the Isle of Dogs. Alternatively, you can walk under the river via the Greenwich Foot Tunnel; it is clean, well-ventilated, has CCTV and lifts. The entrance is by Greenwich Pier.

Whatever route you take, it is a very worthwhile journey to stand where Antonio Canale set up his easel and immortalised for posterity the Greenwich architectural complex in the 1750s. And while his paintbrush famously recorded the glory of the buildings of Wren, Hawksmoor and Vanbrugh, nevertheless it would be the combined efforts of successive Royal Astronomers, diligently noting their observations on the green hill behind, that brought to the world the vital 'kick-start' leading to the eventual calculation of longitude and the universal standardisation of time and date throughout the globe.

The Royal Observatory Greenwich was built more than two and a half centuries before the National Maritime Museum became a reality during the 1930s. The unique site led to the observations in the skies above by the astronomers' achieving GMT and enshrining 'maritime Greenwich' forever as part of our history. John Flamsteed, appointed in 1676 as the first Royal Astronomer, would work and live on the hill for over four decades, laying the foundations for the establishment of Greenwich Mean Time with his formidable and uncompromisingly accurate observations of the movements of the stars. He also installed two remarkable clocks to provide an accurate time-measurement basis for his calculations. This was the initial, official scientific search for longitude, resulting in the publication of the first reliable British *Nautical Almanac* in 1767, just a century after John Flamsteed began his work and a decade or so after Canaletto painted where he did so. It also led to the name of Greenwich becoming forever associated with accurate timekeeping.

Although mechanical clocks were becoming increasingly sophisticated in the 17th century, due to the swing of the pendulum being utilised as a constant and reliable time-measurement span, nevertheless clock-time time would always be different from sundial-time. This was due to the tilt of the Earth, all the while rotating on its axis, and the changing speed of its plane of orbit around the sun. The measurement of sundial time could be up to 16 minutes more or less than that measured by a clock. John Flamsteed, using the two innovatively-designed pendulum clocks at the Royal Observatory, was able to accurately calculate the speed of the rotation of the Earth. Like his successors, he always used time as measured by the stars, otherwise the 'sidereal' time, a term derived from the Latin *sidereus*. A sidereal year was calculated as the time-measurement during which the Earth made one complete revolution around the nearest star, the sun. Accuracy of the speed of the Earth's rotation on its axis was vital for this.

However, for commercial and domestic convenience, as clock technology advanced, the Mean Solar Time Unit came into being when the time of the path of the Earth around the sun was measured for a year; using as a constant the 0.00 degrees of the Greenwich

Meridian – a meridian being the middle of the day north-south reading of the sun's position wherever you are in the world. An average, daily, uniform time-measurement was then calculated to form the basis of Greenwich Local Time; otherwise Greenwich Mean Time. For this we can thank Charles II and his advisers for initiating the building of the Royal Observatory Greenwich on the hill above his intended new palace.

From Island Gardens we can see immediately to the fore, as Canaletto did, the classical buildings begun by Charles II when he was restored to the monarchy in 1660. He intended a complete replacement for the riverside Tudor buildings, by then very dilapidated. He could only afford one stage of what would be the first baroque building in England, the King Charles Court; close inspection of it reveals 'Carolus II' on the upper stonework. His brother, James II, against whom he would pit his navigational skills when racing their yachts alongside on the Thames, probably inspired the future use of the site as a hospital and home for disabled and destitute seamen. His daughter, Queen Mary II, dedicated it as such just before she died of smallpox in 1694.

It would eventually be completed to a very grand design. The ornately Painted Dining Hall in the subsequent King William Court was utilised for the display of naval memorabilia from the 1800s onwards, particularly that formerly belonging to Admiral Horatio Nelson. The expanding collection, which would also include paintings, was destined to become the nucleus of the present National Maritime Museum. Queen Mary II is also afforded the tribute of personally persuading Christopher Wren to leave intact the Queen's House. Built to the rear of the old Tudor palace, it had originally been completed by her grandmother. Apparently with some reluctance, Wren complied. He designed the two small domes for buildings on each side of the house, instead of the one large dome he had envisaged – in the space left after its demolition – possibly to emulate St Paul's Cathedral.

And so the Queen's House remains to this day. To us, from a distance, perhaps resembling an immaculate white dolls' house. In reality, an exquisite Renaissance gem and the first construction of its kind in England; designed in the 1570s by Inigo Jones, the son of a cloth worker who trained as a joiner. When working in Italy he had been much influenced by the crisply-clear proportions of the architecture of Andrea Palladio, who brilliantly created buildings deceptively simple to view outwardly, while inwardly radiating an aura of ordered tranquillity; compositions achieved solely by the application of pure geometry, using simple ratios for 'perfection' and thus thought to be proof of God's existence.

It is recorded that Inigo Jones was mocked for his 'obsession with numbers'. Undeterred, he created the 40 ft (12 metre) cube Great Hall of the Queen's House, occupying two stories. It remains today with magnificent marble floor, gallery and ceiling beams; an outstanding memorial to the workmanship of one who was first employed at the royal court to design masques. The colonnades we now see externally on either side of the Queen's House were added in the early 1800s when the building was used by a naval orphanage; the Neptune Court of the National Maritime Museum is situated in a former gymnasium.

It is perhaps a strange twist of fate that the Greenwich site within a century of Inigo Jones' achievements would be adapted to accommodate the study of mathematics in the skies above, resulting in a destiny then beyond comprehension. For Charles II, we are told, looked up the hill one day from the balcony at the rear of the Queens House and saw the site for a Royal Observatory. He swiftly commissioned it in 1675, prompted by many, particularly the mathematician and astronomer Sir Jonas Moore; also surveyor of the entire length of the River Thames and patron of John Flamsteed who lodged in the Queen's House during the construction of the small redbrick building now named after him.

As we look across the river and obliquely upwards to the right, we can see where John Flamsteed began to do the impossible. From beneath the weather vane on Flamsteed House the orange Time Ball now peeps over the horizon, not unlike a miniature harvest moon. It was one of the world's first visual time signals, achieved a century and a half after John Flamsteed started his observations. A perpetual reminder that it was not until 1833 that the signalling of Greenwich Mean Time begun daily to ships on the Thames below. Then, as now, at 12.55 hours the Time Ball rises halfway up its mast, reaches the top at 12.58 and then drops down exactly at 13.00 hours. It makes a very good photo!

And that ensured safety at sea as never before. The mariners could synchronise their newly developed marine chronometers, perfected to keep accurate Greenwich Mean Time at sea, and so define the life-saving longitude necessary to pinpoint their exact position. For they could at last correctly calculate the distance travelled along a north south line of latitude as the Earth rotated east-west-east through 360 degrees on its axis every twenty-four hours, simply by knowing the correct length of time travelled. Marine chronometry was developed from the invention of the first-ever, accurate, sea-going clock. This was formidably achieved, also over four gruelling decades, by the industrious and dedicated John Harrison. Journeying from Lincolnshire in 1730, he made his way up to the Royal Observatory and confronted Edmund Halley, successor to John Flamsteed, with his revolutionary designs and ideas for the 'Impossible Clock'.

John Harrison would finally perfect his sea-going clock in 1759, but there would be several more frustrating years, regrettably, before his invention was fully approved and commercially adapted for use at sea by a somewhat suspicious Admiralty Board of Longitude, hard put to believe that a problem of such magnitude could be solved by a small round timepiece, five inches in diameter (12.5 cm). For without the reality of swiftly accessible Greenwich Mean Time at sea, the *Cutty Sark,* now proudly dominating the landscape, might never have survived to tell us her story. A short distance downriver from her we can see, from Island Gardens, two white buildings fronting the Thames.

The larger is the popular 18th century Trafalgar Tavern. The smaller quasi-gothic structure that of the 17th century Trinity Hospital almshouses; still in use and nestling, somewhat minutely, beside the four austere chimneys of the electricity generating station built in the early 1900s around the same time as the Greenwich Foot Tunnel. The small glass dome of the northern end of this tunnel is adjacent to where Canaletto painted. The safe building of the Greenwich and also the Woolwich pedestrian tunnels was possible due to the successful construction of the nearby and larger Blackwall Tunnel in the late 19th century. Thus in 1902 the labour force that had for several centuries relied on ferry services, latterly steam, to cross to the dockyards on the Isle of Dogs, could safely walk to work under the river.

It had never been feasible downriver from Tower Hill for the Thames to have bridges erected; it was always a busy thoroughfare especially with the tall ships. As far back as 1390, Geoffrey Chaucer, author of *The Canterbury Tales,* was appointed 'Royal Commissioner for the River between Greenwich and Woolwich' – a particularly interesting stretch of water. In 1624, James I is recorded as witnessing and possibly participating in submarine trials daringly demonstrated to a depth of 12-15 feet (3-4 metres) by its Dutch inventor. On the surface at Millwall, beyond Island Gardens, the innovative steamship, the *Great Eastern* was built. In 1866 she would then successfully complete the laying of the first transatlantic telegraph cable, manufactured and loaded at Greenwich Peninsula.

Greenwich Mean Time would be transmitted around the world by the newly-developed Morse Code. In 1884, a conference in Washington officially confirmed Greenwich as the place where the east-west hemispheres register at 0.00 degrees, otherwise the Prime Meridian. A fact acknowledged unofficially for many decades previously by mariners universally trusting in the *Nautical Almanac* and chronometer. Time zones were officially created with the establishment of twenty-four standard meridians worldwide, each 15 degrees apart, calculated from the 0.00 degrees of the Greenwich Meridian. East and west 'Date Lines' were also established at a longitude of 180 degrees from Greenwich, twelve hours distant in time.

As the 20th century dawned, the internal combustion engine was on the market. The invention of the cathode-ray tube, a vacuum converting electrical signals into black and white images visible on a fluorescent screen, mooted the possibility of television. Homes were routinely wired for electricity. From the 1930s onwards the feasibility of 'thinking machines' were mathematically explored and proven. Clocks were developed using the frequencies of the oscillations, first of quartz crystal in the 1930s and then of atoms in the 1950s, to supersede the swing of the pendulum for assessing time-measurement.

The mechanical computing and storing of information, with the ability to be easily accessed, became a reality. The television monitor could be conveniently attached to a computer programmed with disks containing information, the software. Personal computers and their video screens became universal and commonplace. Rocket power blasted new technology into space. Man made it to the moon and back. The explorations of the skies were relayed down to Earth. Radio-astronomy came into being. Satellite stations were anchored in space. Domestic telephone lines could be utilised for the World Wide Web.

And throughout all these developments ran the vital link of Greenwich Mean Time, determined by astronomical measurements, and Universal Time (UT), determined by atomic clocks. Times zones were sometimes slightly modified to accommodate the large land masses for convenient time reference. Co-ordinated Universal Time, the UTC, adopted as the time given out on radio signals, remains based on Greenwich Mean Time.

An invisible thread for centuries, the Prime Meridian is now denoted from dusk to midnight in the sky over floodlit Greenwich by an emerald-green laser beam, sparkling and especially iridescent in rain; arising from the Meridian Building adjoining Flamsteed House then curving arc-wise down towards the Thames. Beyond and unseen, the Prime Meridian continues down through south-eastern England, France, Spain, north-west Africa via the oceans to Antarctica before converging with all the other lines of longitude at the South Pole.

And just how the Prime Meridian looks at Greenwich can be discovered up in the Royal Observatory. If you want to go straight there with the minimum of effort there is a shuttle bus service direct from outside the Greenwich Pier Office, in the Cutty Sark Gardens. This service is restricted Nov-March. The journey is only five to ten minutes, depending on the traffic, and takes you on a short route through the town centre before passing along the base of the elegantly Georgian Croom's Hill; Greenwich Theatre with its colourful and chequered history is on a corner. Opposite and diagonal to this is the unique and much newer Fan Museum, only a few houses away from the home of Cecil Day Lewis, Poet Laureate, until his death in 1972. Benjamin Waugh, founder of the National Society for the Prevention of Cruelty to Children in 1884 was another noted resident of Croom's Hill.

On turning left into Greenwich Park, a brief but very pleasant ride transports you up The Avenue to the Royal Observatory complex, comprising Flamsteed House, the Meridian Building and the Planetarium. Below and to the rear of the Royal Observatory are the secluded Castle Hill Gardens; convenient for picnics, but not a designated area for such. Access, however, is only available from the park and The Avenue.

In line with the Royal Observatory, two hundred yards or so across the park to the west is the superb Ranger's House. Macartney House, the family home of General Wolfe of Quebec is adjacent. Famous for his conquest of the Heights of Abraham culminating in the surrender of Montreal in 1760, General Wolfe's statue by the Canadian sculptor Tait Mackenzie now enjoys the panoramic view at the front of the Royal Observatory. Erected by the Canadian people in 1930, it was unveiled by a direct descendent of his old adversary. The plinth bears the battle scars of WWII when damaged by a flying bomb which also destroyed part of the dome at the Royal Observatory.

To the rear lies Blackheath Common with an area of around 267 acres (107 hectares). The ancient pastime of bowls remains a regular feature on the pristine green outside Ranger's House. Not far away is the Royal Blackheath Golf Club, possibly owing its origins to the court of James VI of Scotland when he inherited the throne from Elizabeth I. His entourage is thought likely to have brought the game south.

The area of Blackheath remained in Kent until the County of London was formed in 1889. The Metropolitan Boroughs of Greenwich and Woolwich amalgamated to become the London Borough of Greenwich in 1965. The present population of the environs of the UNESCO World Heritage Site is approximately 250,000; the area covers over eighteen square miles (46 Sq Km) with a river boundary of seven miles (12 Km). The Borough also includes Charlton, Eltham, Woolwich, Plumstead and parts of Deptford and Blackheath. Blackheath Common is steeped in history and not a little notoriety for it would be the rallying ground for the unsuccessful Peasants' Revolt, demonstrating against the Poll Tax and corruption in 1381; led by Wat Tyler from Kent and Jack Straw storming the supposedly impregnable Tower of London.

Also unsuccessful was the Kentish Rebellion of 1450 when Jack Cade and his 40,000 followers with their list of grievances, the 'Blackheath Petition', marched down to London to present it to the monarch. Nearly fifty years later some 6000 Cornish rebels, discontented at having to pay taxes to finance wars with Scotland, would be defeated by Henry VII at Blackheath in 1497. Exactly five hundred years later, in June 1997, a plaque commemorating their stand, inscribed in both the English and Cornish languages, was unveiled by the London Cornish Association near the Park Office by Blackheath Gate.

The name of Blackheath was possibly derived from use as a burial ground for plague victims. Certainly, the Anglo-Saxons left behind a selection of some thirty burial mounds dated around AD 650 near Croom's Hill, not far from the area that would be enclosed as Greenwich Park. It would be the first royal park and created by Duke

Humphrey of Gloucester, brother of Henry V. Initially stocked with a hundred deer from Essex, a Park Keeper was appointed in 1486. Previously, on his return from Agincourt in 1415, Henry V had been greeted on Blackheath by the Lord Mayor and citizens of London, but without triumphal rejoicing at his request

Today, further across the park to the east from the Royal Observatory, the legacy of the once royal hunting ground lives on; conserved as a protected wildlife pond and deer park, 'The Wilderness'. Delightful picnic spots can be found in the beautiful multi-bedded flower and rose gardens, surrounded by magnificent shady cedars and rare trees. A stroll further eastwards from the iron bandstand made by the Coalbrookdale Company in 1891 brings you to a much older small area, confirmed by excavations in 1902 and 1979 to be the site of a Celtic-Roman temple, considered first century AD. Many coins were found, some very rare and suggesting the possibility of financial offerings to deities.

Beyond are Maze Hill and the red-brown brick turrets and green spire of Vanbrugh Castle. This is the only survivor of the several Gothic-type mansion follies built on the hill by architect and Restoration Comedy dramatist, Sir John Vanbrugh. He succeeded Christopher Wren as Surveyor of Greenwich Hospital in 1716. One opinion is that the building was supposed to resemble Greenwich Castle, previously on the site of the Royal Observatory. Later it would be a school until 1977 when divided into four private residences.

Although not apparently having any formal training as an architect, Sir John Vanbrugh is also credited with the designing, albeit aided by Nicholas Hawksmoor and Christopher Wren, of Castle Howard in Yorkshire and Blenheim Palace in Oxfordshire. Various other notable commissions also survive; the style was given the accolade 'English Baroque'. Reputedly a jovial and expansive personality, Sir John Vanbrugh lived as a child in Chester. He was the son of a sugar baker; perhaps even influenced by that craft in his future architectural flamboyance. His grandfather, Gillis van Brugg, was a prosperous and respected merchant in Ghent who fled to England to avoid religious persecution.

The Flemish origins of Sir John Vanbrugh are coincidental to Greenwich's political and religious ties with Ghent which relate back to the 10th century. For in AD 871 King Alfred, of burnt cakes notoriety but much wisdom otherwise for his realm, inherited the lands of Greenwich. His father, Egbert, had already established the supremacy of Wessex over a then-just-united England. Until quite recently it has been considered likely that Alfred handed on this inheritance of the fishing hamlets of Greenwich and Woolwich (otherwise *Gronewic* and *Wuluuich*) plus Lewisham to his daughter, Princess Elstrudis, when she married the Count of Flanders, Baldwin II. Later, when widowed, she was presumed to have donated them to the Abbey of St Peter in Ghent around 918 AD.

However, documents relating to these transactions are now considered forgeries; possibly by the monks themselves as a smokescreen. The view is now held that King Edgar, who acceded to the English throne in 959 AD, granted a Royal Charter to the monks at St Peter's Abbey in gratitude for sanctuary given to the exiled Bishop Dunstan four years earlier. Whatever the reasons, there was a very strong contingent of monks at Greenwich engaging in a constant two-way traffic of business to Flanders, until Henry V confiscated their rights in 1414 by disallowing 'possession of alien monasteries'. Their property from then on belonged to the Crown; the Manor of Greenwich was created. A few Franciscan Friars remained for a century under considerable sufferance, baptising Henry VIII and marrying him to his first wife, Catherine of Aragon. Their opposition to his later demands to divorce her led to their virtual extinction.

Only eight years after their first banishment, the young King Henry V had died in 1422. Acting as regent, Duke Humphrey rebuilt the riverside manor he had inherited, named it 'Bellacourt' and enclosed 200 acres of 'pasture, wood, heath, virses (furse) and gorse thereof' to make Greenwich Park. A few years later, in 1427, this highly intelligent and far-sighted veteran of Agincourt built a small tower on the hill in Greenwich Park to guard the south-eastern approaches to London. It would have many uses during the next two centuries until the Royal Observatory was built on the original foundations in 1672; an event which would no doubt have delighted him.

Duke Humphrey was a renowned scholar and after his rather suspicious death in prison at Bury St Edmunds in 1447, his extensive and valuable archives were bequeathed to Oxford University. This gift would later form the nucleus of the Bodleian Library developed there by the 16th century scholar and diplomat, Thomas Bodley. The Greenwich estate, honourably or otherwise, then came into the possession of Margaret of Anjou, who renamed it 'Palace of Pleasaunce'. Disliked by many, including Duke Humphrey, she was the wife of his nephew Henry VI. Their son, Henry VII, was the grandfather of Elizabeth I. She was also a lover of scholarship and Greenwich Park. When walking through today you may pass a massive hollowed oak tree, now lying aslant on the ground. Elizabeth I's ill-starred parents, Henry VIII and Ann Boleyn, are reputed to have cavorted around it in their heyday. The small oak growing nearby was planted by Prince Philip, Baron Greenwich, to commemorate 40 years reign of Queen Elizabeth II.

The Tudor Queen Elizabeth I would reign for forty-five years. Legend relates that she herself took shelter from a storm in the massive oak tree, when not sitting nearby on One Tree Hill and admiring the views. Now, down to the right from One Tree Hill she would see a children's play area and the Boating Pond by Park Row Gate; nearby on the approach from Romney Road are some anchors, including that of the former royal yacht *Victoria and Albert*.

Greenwich Park has approximately eleven gates, generous paths and many signposts. From the gate in Park Row, you can follow the wide herbaceous border along to the Queen's House and beyond. Just before you reach the *al fresco* area of the Regatta Café at the National Maritime Museum, there is a strip of garden planted with rosemary, purple sage, golden yew and peace roses. A bronze plaque above a small plinth of Cornish granite, traditionally used as ballast, denotes the dedication in 1995 by a survivor of the *RMS Titanic* which sank in 1912 when Mrs Edith Haisman was fifteen years old.

Close by is the Queen Elizabeth II Silver Jubilee Sundial, elegant in its simplicity and ingenuously portraying the time of day from the shadows cast by the tails of the dancing dolphins; sculpted by Edwin Russell and designed by Christopher Daniel, who was on the staff of the National Maritime Museum from 1964-86. Their work faces the Jubilee Tree Avenue sloping gently upwards to the moderately steep approach to the Royal Observatory. To the rear in an alcove can be seen a large bust of Horatio Nelson, commissioned by William IV and sculpted by Sir Francis Chantrey.

When Charles II had the park landscaped in the mid-17th century with 6000 elms and Spanish chestnuts, a series of 'Giant Steps' were created to lead down from the hill. They would become known as the Tumbling Steps, the site of much feisty merriment when the great fairs were held in Greenwich Park from 1838-57 at Easter and Whitsuntide. Charles Dickens would eloquently describe them as

"A three-day fever which cools the blood for six months afterwards..."

It is on record that fifty steamers carried 150,000 revellers daily to a new Greenwich Pier, opened in 1836. There was also, we are told, 'unseemly dancing' in public. However, you may prefer to take your pleasure more sedately by wandering and enjoying the oaks, planes, chestnuts and other rare trees that remained after the Great Storm of 1987. A total of some 350 were then destroyed.

This recently designated UNESCO World Heritage Site has already survived for six centuries, witnessing and participating in momentous change. We can explore all that is on offer at Greenwich as we wish. There is no shortage of amenities. You will not get lost. If you have come 'on the hop' or uncharacteristically left your sandwiches behind, you will not go hungry. Enjoy it all!

The entrance to the National Maritime Museum, Romney Road (Author)

Life-size statue of Peter the Great at Millennium Quay, Deptford, on plinth supplied by Russian Quarry, commemorating his visit in 1698 to study shipbuilding. Donated in 2001 by Sculptor Mikhail Cheniakin and presented by Prince Michael of Kent. (Author)

29

Flamsteed House showing the Time Ball

The Time Ball. The ball rises up its mast to drop at exactly 13.00hrs. Ships on the Thames could set their chronometers to GMT by this signal.

(Author)

Ancient and modern. The exterior of the chapel with the Canary Wharf development visible across the river from Romney Rd.
(Author)

The Queens House and Greenwich Park, south side.
(Author)

The Cutty Sark. The bow Figurehead (above) and the stern.

(Author)

Below is the memorial to the Merchant Navy in the days of sail.

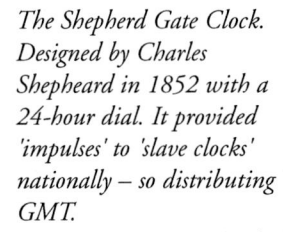

The Shepherd Gate Clock. Designed by Charles Shepheard in 1852 with a 24-hour dial. It provided 'impulses' to 'slave clocks' nationally – so distributing GMT.

(Author)

THE CUTTY SARK

> *"They mark our passage as a race of men,*
> *Earth will not see such ships again."*
>
> (From *Ships* by John Masefield, Poet Laureate 1930-67,
> and inscribed on a bench in the Cutty Sark Gardens.)

The *Cutty Sark's* unusual name can be traced to the Scotland of Robert Burns and his famous poem, *Tam O'Shanter*, relating the ancient legend of a drunken farmer riding past a blazing church surrounded by witches and then being pursued by the youngest and most beautiful, Nannie. She was clad in a short shift of Paisley linen, a 'cutty sark'. Nannie would hold onto the tail of Tam's mare until it came off in her hand approaching the bridge at Doon. Witches could not cross running water. Today the beautiful figurehead of the clipper ship illustrates the legend; the voluptuous carving reaching out towards Greenwich Pier today has the left arm extended, the fingers outstretched and clutching at a thick strand of horsehair.

The *Cutty Sark* was superbly and innovatively designed initially for the tea trade and launched in 1869; unfortunately around the time of the building of the Suez Canal. As a result the sea routes to the Orient would be drastically shortened; the installation of coaling stations would confirm the superiority of steam over sail. The success of the subsequent steam ship era guaranteed we had our favourite brew quicker, but within a few years quite simply 'took the wind out of the sails' of the *Cutty Sark*, and those of her class: they were built to 'clip the waves' with great speed while carrying relatively limited cargoes.

The importing and selling of tea in England is dated back to 1657. Introduced by the East India Company, it was initially sold at the almost prohibitively expensive four guineas per pound (0.5 Kg). With the restoration of the monarchy three years later, Charles II's Portuguese wife, Catherine of Braganza, would further popularise it. Tea buyers and brokers had their offices in Mincing Lane in the City of London and operated in China via agents. The tea was grown in smallholdings, packed in chests made of local wood and ferried down to the Treaty Ports in the small traditional craft of the Chinese, the sampan.

There would eventually be some two thousand of the rather ambiguously named 'Tea Merchant's Coffee Houses' in London. The drinking of tea remained very expensive until the late 18th century when a young Prime Minister, William Pitt, reduced the tax on it from 119% to $12^{1}/2$% when reforming the fiscal system. This substantially controlled the smuggling of tea and encouraged the fashionable, non-alcoholic and remedial beverage to become very affordable and universally socially acceptable. The Victorian premier, William Gladstone, reputedly had his stone hot water bottles filled with it and put in his bed to quench his thirst during the night. An enterprising tea merchant, the Quaker John Horniman, pioneered the packaging of unadulterated tea into convenient amounts for the consumer and devoted most of his considerable profits to philanthropy. The last weekly Tea Auction in the City of London took place as recently as June 1998.

In the days of the *Cutty Sark*, 130 million pounds of tea (60 million Kg) would be shipped to England annually. The first shipment home had greatly enhanced value and although never actually winning a tea race from Shanghai to London, the *Cutty Sark* often outran a unique class of sister vessel. Her passage back from China varied according to winds and was between 107 and 122 days. On outgoing voyages, the holds were filled with textiles and supplies of metals and heavy gear for railways. The average cargo weighed 1,375,364 pounds (623,835 Kg). Although the *Cutty Sark* only participated in the great annual Shanghai Tea Races from 1870-77, she more than proved her worth when transferring to the wool runs from Australia for twelve years. A cargo of wool could be worth £100,000 then. Her fastest voyage to England took 72 days in 1885, via the dreaded Cape Horn.

In 1895, when the wool runs were no longer viable, the *Cutty Sark* was sold and for twenty-seven years sailed under the Portuguese flag, being renamed twice. First as the *Ferreira*, otherwise known endearingly to her crews as the *Pequina Camisola* or 'little shirt' and secondly as the *Maria do Amparo*. When spars were scarce during World War I she was converted to a barquentine – only the foremast of this class had square-rigged sails.

During 1922 she was driven by bad weather into Falmouth, Cornwall, where despite her change of name and appearance she was recognised, fortuitously, by an old admirer, Captain Wilfred Dowman. He had seen her sailing, unforgettably, at full speed when an apprentice nearly three decades before. For the sum of £3,750 Captain Dowman bought her back from Portugal. The *Cutty Sark* was reborn and refitted. Later, his widow donated her as a training ship. When no longer required for this purpose, she was painstakingly restored and is now maintained by the Maritime Trust as a permanent memorial to the Merchant Navy of the days of sail in peacetime.

The *Cutty Sark*'s strong slender keel no longer rests on the waves, but on the concrete of her small dry dock beside Greenwich Pier. She has remained ceaselessly intriguing and enchanting to her millions of visitors. Her beautiful construction, with a squarer stern than her rivals, allowed more sail to be accommodated and also ensured extra stability; but the very economic costing at £17 per ton (1016 Kg) totalled £16,150 and regrettably ruined the firm that undertook her contract, Scott and Linton of Dumbarton, near Glasgow, Scotland.

The granddaughter of her young and talented designer, Hercules Linton, would later loan his original sketches and the sail and rigging plan for her restoration in the early 1950s. These were complemented by the general plans and notebooks from the descendents of the chief draughtsman and the first ship's carpenter. The amidships section is believed to have been inspired by the shape of the fishing boats in the Firth of Forth, the estuary of the 50 mile long (80 Km) river flowing from central Scotland into the North Sea.

Despite the 'tween decks giving her extra rigidity, the *Cutty Sark* was twice relieved of her rudder during typhoons in the Indian Ocean, and once of her mast.

The frame was iron and the spars of Oregon pine. During construction, rock elm planking 11 in thick (28 cm) was laid over with teak 4.6 in thick (12 cm). The highest quality control was insisted on by her first commander, Captain George Moodie, no doubt leading to the vessel's longevity. In all, the *Cutty Sark* carried square sails on three masts; the mainmast stands 155 ft high (47 m), the lower foremast 85 ft (26 m). The total complement of twenty-nine sails had a canvas spread of 32,000 sq ft (2,972 Sq m) accommodated on 11 miles of rigging (18 Km).

It is said that when fully rigged the sails covered an area equivalent to that of eleven tennis courts and that the *Cutty Sark*'s rate of performance was equivalent to that of 2,250 horsepower (550 foot-pounds per second) and generated a speed of 17 knots, otherwise 19.5 mph (31.5 kph). With an overall length of 280 ft (85 m) a beam of 35 ft (11 m), and a moulded depth of 23 ft (7 m), the gross tonnage totalled 936 tons (978.5 tonnes). In order to calculate Greenwich Mean Time at sea and estimate her correct position, the *Cutty Sark* depended on Chronometer Number 4608, made by a firm established in Liverpool in 1800 by Joseph Sewell. He would eventually be appointed as 'Chronometer, Watch and Nautical Instrument Manufacturer to the Right Honourable the Lords Commissioners of the Admiralty'.

With her course set, apparently there was time for lighter moments aboard the *Cutty Sark*. The redoubtable Captain Woodget, commander 1885-1895, was renowned for learning to ride a bicycle in an empty hold and for wearing his carpet slippers on the main deck; this apparently remained dry even in the tumultuous seas of the southern hemisphere. He would also write that: "Captains do not like to admit that the Cutty Sark can sail, and yet not one of them can show that she has ever been beaten by any sailing vessel that has left London or Sydney about the same time".

Now, up on her great main deck beneath the mighty mast strung with the multitudinous rigging and surrounded by windlass, cathead tackles, a capstan and a bowsprit seemingly to ride higher than Canary Wharf opposite, it is hard not to capture the aura of pride that inspired the *Cutty Sark* amid the perils of the South China Seas and Indian Ocean.

Artefacts from those tremendous times can be seen in the main exhibition on the 'tween deck, now our point of entry. Soon on view are the great tea chests labelled 'black' and 'green'; the colour is dependent on the method of drying. Nearby is the original 'cutty sark' metal emblem, once worn on the main mast. It was dramatically rescued from a London saleroom in 1960 and is now displayed along with a copy of the original registration certificate, archives and other riveting memorabilia including two superb models.

From the 'tween deck it is possible to glimpse into the hold area, without having to negotiate the steep stairs down to it. Resplendently, the Long John Silver Collection of figureheads from merchant ships now takes the place of cargo, donated by Captain John Cumbers of Gravesend; a small town twenty-five miles downstream and once a Saxon settlement supplying river pilots. In striking contrast to the bold colours and stimulating torsos of the figureheads, with names ranging from *Old Goody* to *Maude* and *Gladstone* to *Disraeli*, there is also on display a fascinating array of seamen's tools and the exquisite carving of *Golden Cherubs* attributed to the Rotterdam-born Grinling Gibbons.

Throughout the *Cutty Sark* the attention given to her imaginative refurbishment is meticulously detailed and evocatively presents a seemingly effortless and encyclopaedic knowledge of how her crew of twenty-eight, including eight boys, fared in a tough and bygone age. The ordinary seamen's spartan quarters are both a visual and audio logbook, sometime humorous, of daily life aboard. The saloon, which doubled as a chart room, has beautifully gilded carved teak and bird's-eye-maple panelling. Decanters, an open fireplace and blue willow-pattern china – oriental porcelain was used as ballast for the 'tubbs' of tea – make for homely touches in what must have been a rigorous, and at times an extremely hazardous, existence for all ranks. One fine master, Captain Wallace, voluntarily committed himself to the depths of the South Seas in 1880 to avoid mutiny when a malevolent Mate committed murder aboard and was, questionably, allowed safe passage on another vessel.

Today, a few yards from the bows of the *Cutty Sark* can be found the miniscule *Gipsy Moth IV*, which the English yachtsman Sir Francis Chichester sailed alone for 226 days single-handedly round the world in 1967. Complete with a barrel of ale in the tiny galley to celebrate his 65th birthday aboard and seeds of mustard and cress, apparently nurtured to prevent scurvy. *Gipsy Moth IV* was purpose-built in 1966, in Hampshire, England, at a cost of £35,000 to discover whether a fast modern vessel could make a return passage to Australia with only a solo crew in the same time, or less, as the racing clippers of the *Cutty Sark* era. Although this target was not quite achieved, it was the fastest voyage around the world made by any small boat at that time. Not only breaking the record for a single-handed week's run by more than 100 miles (160 Km), but also for covering a distance of 1400 miles sailed (2253 Km) in eight days. In all a total of 29,630 miles of ocean (47,680 Km) were covered from Plymouth to Sydney and back.

On his return, Francis Chichester was knighted by the Queen in the Grand Square of the Old Royal Naval College, adjacent to the Cutty Sark Gardens. Some of the college buildings are now leased to Greenwich University; another, incorporating the independent Greenwich Maritime Institute, is dedicated to the future needs of the global maritime community. Using the same sword in 1580, Queen Elizabeth I had likewise honoured Francis Drake on his return from sailing round the world, the first Englishman to do so, after setting off down the Thames three years previously. It is alleged that Drake's return home fanfare salute blew out some of the windows in Elizabeth I's riverside palace, alongside the present Cutty Sark Gardens. She knighted him upriver at Deptford on the quarterdeck of the *Golden Hinde*, the renamed *Pelican*, and was later obliged to spend a large portion of her 'cut' of his very substantial booty to help finance the Spanish Armada in 1588.

Even further upriver today, a very reliably researched authentic replica of Drake's ship is anchored in the tranquil and minute St Mary Overie Dock, cleft between the modern office buildings by Southwark Cathedral, and well worth a visit. The original *Golden Hinde* was a tourist attraction and also a venue for banquets at Deptford for nearly a century before disintegrating; some of her timbers were saved and made into a few items of furniture that still exist scattered in various museums and buildings.

It is to be hoped that the *Cutty Sark* does not meet with the same fate, for her fabric is deteriorating dangerously, particularly as the rock elm planking shrinks in dry dock. Other further conservation is imperative and expensive. The splendid 'gingerbread' decoration on her stern, below the Star of India, boasts the motto of her inspirer, 'White-Hat' John Willis: 'Where there's a Will is a Way'.

Just below, on the rear wall of the dry dock and approachable by steps, is the large memorial tribute to 'the ships and men of the merchant navy in days of sail'. Carved in stone, it was erected by the Cutty Sark Preservation Society in 1954, dedicated in the presence of the Patron, the Duke of Edinburgh.

The *Cutty Sark* has previously been saved from destruction. It is nearly fifty years since her last restoration when she returned to Greenwich; not to the north side of the Thames where she had often berthed at the East India Dock, built in 1614 by Blackwall, but to her present permanent anchorage on the site of several 'Ship' taverns built on the waterfront at Greenwich from the 16th century onwards. The origin of the taverns is almost as fascinating as that of the *Cutty Sark*'s.

Inigo Jones, acknowledged as the founder of the English classical school of architecture, when not building the Queen's House at Greenwich and the Banqueting House in Whitehall among others, bought a tavern in Greenwich. His reasons for this are unknown. He was, however, deeply concerned with the restriction and regulation of new buildings in London where fire was a particularly constant threat. Possibly he had misgivings about the congested riverside area in Greenwich, where he was often resident. However, he sold the Blew Boar almost immediately to Henry Howard, the Earl of Arundel, founder of the Trinity Hospital almshouse for '21 Gentlemen of Greenwich' a few hundred yards downriver.

Later, another busy citizen and resident of Greenwich, William Smith, also Sergeant-at-Arms to Charles I, rebuilt on the extended inn site and renamed the Blew Boar; the first of the 'Ship' taverns came into being. The 'Ship' taverns would become particularly famous for whitebait suppers, along with the Trafalgar tavern. Greenwich was a very popular and enjoyable place in which to eat. Samuel Pepys was eloquent on the subject. Various fish dishes were also served in the many other hostelries.

Greenwich fishermen had traditionally sailed at Easter to Iceland and the Faroes, returning at the end of the summer with their catches. When Grimsby expanded at the mouth of the Humber, the Greenwich fishermen emigrated to north Lincolnshire and took advantage of the steam trawling introduced around 1881. The fourth 'Ship' tavern was by all accounts a very splendid Victorian building, inside and out. The chandeliers were designed for the Great Exhibition at Hyde Park in 1851. Leading politicians, including that supposed soul of sobriety, Prime Minister Gladstone, would sail downriver at the end of each summer recess to indulge in their whitebait suppers at Greenwich. However, decline set in and the last and very much smaller 'Ship' tavern was destroyed by a direct hit during the blitzes on London's dockland in World War II.

But like a phoenix rising from the ashes, a decade or so later, the *Cutty Sark*'s ensign would be hoisted aloft over the site and hopefully will continue to do so for many a year to come.

THE PAINTED DINING HALL AND CHAPEL THE OLD ROYAL NAVAL COLLEGE

formerly

THE ROYAL HOSPITAL FOR SEAMEN

> *"The relief and support of seamen aboard the ships and vessels belonging to the Royal Navy…who by reason of age, wound or other disabilities shall be incapable of further service at sea and be unable to maintain themselves…"*
>
> (The Charter of Foundation, 1692, drawn up after the victory of the British over Louis XIV of France.)

The former Royal Hospital for Seamen, magnificent in Portland stone and marble, was built with great dedication and the very considerable cost of £400,000, over a period of 50 years. The imposing West Gate, adjacent to the *Cutty Sark* and the Visitor and Information Centre, is flanked by pillars with two stone globes aloft; representing the celestial and terrestrial spheres while also commemorating the circumnavigation of the world by *HMS Centurion* in the mid-1700s.

On the immediate right of the West Gate is the former Infirmary to the Royal Hospital, later the Dreadnought Hospital for Seamen and specialising in research on tropical diseases. It was badly damaged during World War II and recently restored by the University of Greenwich as a library, while retaining the name of the original hospital ship once moored off Greenwich.

A few minutes walk beyond on the right will bring you to the King William and Queen Mary Courts, easily discerned by Wren's domes and housing the Painted Dining Hall and Chapel. You enter by the undercroft. A short sweep of wide shallow stairs will guide you to the famously-painted Dining Hall in King William Court. The flamboyant scenario of classical, royal and religious figures allegorically floating among billowing clouds denoting Peace and Liberty, the Zodiac and Time, enhanced by an enormous frieze and Latin mottos, was achieved over a period of nineteen years by James Thornhill, who began it when aged thirty-two. The ceiling of the lower section, measuring 108 x 50 ft (33 x 15.5 m) and 50 ft high, took five years to paint. The cost was £3 per square yard (0.8 Sq m) for the ceiling and £1 for the walls. A total and rather modest sum, even then, of £6,685.

What could be considered, perhaps, the extravaganza of the Painted Hall is always astounding to the eye, particularly when brilliantly illuminated by the candelabras for evening functions. Then the long refectory tables, agleam with the silver plate for several hundred diners, provide a brilliant contrast to the rich subtle hues of the artist's palette so liberally bestowed on the walls and ceilings of the Upper and Lower Halls. But not by any means could the baroque splendour be envisaged as a 'cosy' environment for elderly seamen used to messing in cramped quarters aboard or boarding in simple friendly lodging houses ashore. One outspoken criticism, recorded in 1771, was that 'Columns, colonnades and friezes ill accord with bully beef and sour beer mixed with water'. The old salts took to eating elsewhere in the building; one brighter area favoured was that below the Painted Hall, now the Wardroom Restaurant and providing a very different fare.

Before leaving the Painted Hall you will see, on the right and inlaid in the floor, a memorial and roll of honour with the tribute that 'On 15 June 1941 three citizens of the USA, the first of their countrymen, became officers of the Royal Navy.' Nearby, Horatio Nelson had lain in state on an elevated dais surrounded by sombre funeral splendour. Albeit having been brought home preserved in brandy aboard *HMS Victory* from Trafalgar Cape off Gibraltar, after trouncing Napoleon's ships and dispelling that dictator's dreams forever of invading Britain.

Nelson's last voyage up the Thames was in his flagship's barge before he anchored forever on 8 January 1806, in St Paul's Cathedral as he wished. It is recorded that 500 pensioners marched behind as he was carried out of the Painted Hall. Soon after Nelson's death the Painted Hall housed a small naval museum with many of his effects; visitors were often shown around by the residents. By the 1830s the lower windows were bricked in and the walls covered with paintings. By 1850 the National Gallery of Naval Art had been established there. There is a painting of *Nelson's Funeral on the Thames* by Daniel Turner in the London Maritime Gallery in Neptune Court at the NMM. It was not until 1938 that the Painted Hall was used again for dining; thrice daily by the personnel of the Royal Naval College for the next sixty years.

When finally departing for the now combined army-navy-air college at Cranwell in Lincolnshire, the Royal Naval College's White Ensign was fittingly last struck on 21 October 1998, Trafalgar Day, at the closing ceremony marking their one hundred and twenty year stay. It now hangs in the octagonal vestibule at the main entrance to the Chapel, opposite the Painted Hall, in Queen Mary II Court. A short stroll across the green will bring you there, affording an excellent view en route of the Queen's House, as seen across Romney Road. Alternatively, you can remain indoors and go via the Chalk Walk below, in the basement undercroft linking the two courts and where the seamen once played at skittles. The walls are illustrated with small topical portraits and paintings. Refreshments can be obtained in the evocatively furnished Queen Mary Ante-room occupying the large space beneath the Chapel.

The Chapel today commemorates the lost of the wars of the 20th century. There are Books of Remembrance for the Convoys and WRNS in World War II. The gilded marble altar slab is dedicated to naval chaplains; the candlesticks to members of Lloyds. Within the cable-design mosaic of the marble floor, a central medallion denotes an anchor encircled by a compass rose. The east end is dominated by the American-born artist Benjamin West's painting, *The Preservation of St Paul after Shipwreck at Malta*, above the altar. The dark solemnity of this large work is both offset and enhanced by the effect of spaciousness throughout. This is encouraged by the rectangular design, flat ceiling and extensive Rococo decoration in clear, fragile hues, incorporating a myriad of minutely detailed designs accentuated by a raised 'cameo effect'. Some of the larger mouldings in the chapel were very authentically contrived with the synthetic Coade Stone.

Restoration was carried out in 1980 and the appearance today is very light, bright and fresh. Public worship is encouraged, there is frequent use for concerts and sometimes as a film set; the second nuptials in 'Four Weddings and A Funeral' was located here. The Corinthian pillars and the organ gallery railings are made of *scagliola*, an amalgam of plaster and glue; they are very effectively painted to resemble marble, for economy. However, the 18th century organ, built by Samuel Green, is encased in genuine Spanish mahogany.

It was not until twenty years after the death of Christopher Wren that his design for the Chapel was finally completed with the aid of the Yorkshireman Thomas Ripley; initially a carpenter and then protégé of the Prime Minister, Sir Robert Walpole. After destruction in 1779 by fire in the tailor's shop spreading upwards from the undercroft, the Chapel was rebuilt and redecorated by devotee of the classical world, James 'Athenian' Stuart and the lesser-known William Newton.

Leaving the chapel will bring you out again into the Grand Square; just opposite are the Courts of Queen Anne and King Charles I fronting the river. The four courts were all begun by Christopher Wren and completed by his associates. The foundation stone was laid by Wren. The ceremony is recorded as taking place on 30 June 1696 with Mr John Flamsteed, Royal Astronomer, in attendance with his instruments and calculating the time at "precisely five in the evening".

The treasurer for building the project, John Evelyn, was appointed when in his mid-seventies; an astute gesture, as it proved, for several more years. Generously, he contributed £1,000; half of the monarch's own donation and never drew the salary to which he was entitled. Christopher Wren gave some of his services for free and began adding to the then sole King Charles Block, begun in 1664 by John Webb to be the King's House. Charles II had been allowed £50,000 on his Restoration in 1660 but the Court of the Stuarts was extravagant. The money ran out for further building.

During the Great Plague of 1665-6, the King Charles Block was converted temporarily to naval offices and occupied by Samuel Pepys in his role as administrator; but his diary records rather a "merry time down at Greenwich". Wren extended the building as the King Charles Court; now leased by the Greenwich Foundation to the Trinity School of Music.

The compound of the Old Royal Seamen's Hospital is also often used for film locations; the palatial buildings are very similar to Whitehall. We are told that when the supply of Portland stone began dwindling, for Wren was also building St Paul's Cathedral, further supplies were obtained by Nicholas Hawksmoor in Kent and Yorkshire. Daniel Defoe, who published *Robinson Crusoe* in 1719, but was less lucky in business, also contributed from his venture with a brick-and-tile works at Tilbury. Financial back-up came from many sources including the 'Chatham Chest', a charitable fund for seamen set up in 1590 and built up from the sixpence (5p) deducted monthly from their wages. From 1696, another sixpence per month was deducted. French merchants caught smuggling had their fines donated in 1697, amounting to £10,500.

Parliament provided £6,000 per year raised from the Coal Tax. All unclaimed naval prize money from captured enemy vessels was contributed along with the proceeds of a special lottery – not normally allowed. The then Ranger of the Park, Lord Romney, forfeited his financial right to establish a market in Greenwich. Queen Anne, who succeeded the joint reign of her sister Queen Mary II and King William III of Orange, in 1712 donated to the hospital building funds the princely sum of £6,472 and a shilling. This was retrieved as the ill-gotten gains of a certain Scottish-born, portly and middle-aged Captain William Kidd. He met his nemesis for charges of piracy and murder in the Execution Dock at Wapping in 1701, not far across the Thames from Deptford where he originally set sail.

The wreck of his vessel, *Adventure Galley*, is now considered by some to be off a small island near Madagascar and hiding a booty of possibly £70 million. A respected sea captain, ship owner and otherwise pillar of society in New York, he apparently turned to 'illegal piracy', became the terror of the Indian Ocean and appeared to have betrayed the trust of his official sponsors to defend the ships of the East India Company. We can only surmise the reasons.

The Indian Ocean was no doubt an area familiar to many of the sailors who came to Greenwich from 1705 onwards. Also known, too, by Francis Drake who, despite being the son of a one-time preacher at Chatham Dockyard, temporarily 'excommunicated' his chaplain in the Spice Islands when grounded onto a reef. Six tons of cloves had to be jettisoned.

If Drake sailed up the Thames Estuary today he might be forgiven for being confused at the sight of the Thames Flood Barrier at Woolwich, but continuing upriver to Greenwich he would no doubt be pleased to see what was built in place of the Tudor palace he knew so well. Old age would elude him; he died of fever in the West Indies aged fifty-six.

It is without question that much was done by the Royal Hospital for Seamen from its instigation until finally closing in 1869 to alleviate the condition of many. The tragic plight of the destitute elderly and injured seamen, and soldiers, begging on the streets and forced to exist in squalid huddles, had greatly worried many as the diaries and records relate.

Accommodation was initially for 2000 peaking to 2700 in 1814. According to records, the pensioners were allotted 'cabins' 7 ft square (0.6 Sq m); these they could decorate as they wished. The dormitories were mostly open plan, but with curtains for some privacy. Many preferred not to be too isolated. Two clean white shirts a week were provided in summer and there was also a small allowance, 'tobacco money'. Some could supplement this by showing visitors around the Painted Hall, caddying for golfers on Blackheath and renting out telescopes in Greenwich Park. Apparently, the sighting of criminals, post-execution and bobbing on the tide was a ghoulish amusement for some visitors. Probably neither of those indefatigable telescope users, John Flamsteed onerously recording the movement of the stars in the Royal Observatory all night nor Christopher Wren who enjoyed 'chasing comets across the evening sky', would have condoned such frivolous usage of the newly-found instruments of science!

The refuge was, however, a vast place to administer and as such, brought considerable problems at times with staffing and stairs. Particularly, boredom and loss of purpose in life were noted. A library and reading-room was not provided until 1828; maybe it had not been thought necessary until then. Residents included all races. In 1759 Briton Hamilton dictated his autobiography there, the first, apparently, of a black man in the UK. Greenwich had for centuries been cosmopolitan; some of the ethnic citizens neither servant nor slave, as parish records reveal. It is considered that these people may possibly have been descendents of the retinue of staff Catherine of Aragon brought with her from Spain, on her first ill-fated marriage to Prince Arthur; later she would marry his brother Henry VIII and be a much-loved queen consort of the nation for some twenty years, until the disaster of her estrangement in 1533, leading to the Reformation. She died in 1536.

Gradually, the numbers of pensioners declined. Trafalgar was the last major sea battle that century. It became possible to receive the food and other allowances in cash; this benefited those with families who could remain living at home. Victorian Greenwich expanded and industries developed. Pollution became a problem. The influx of nearly 3000 elderly persons was a lot to contain in any small town at any time. The Seamen's Hospital, having served its purpose, closed in 1869. Four years later, after some adaptations, the Naval College at Portsmouth and School of Naval Architecture and Marine

Engineering from Kensington transferred there; combined as the Royal Naval College. Controversially at first, it became the Royal Navy's very own 'university of much mathematics and science'.

The aftermath of the Battle of Trafalgar would provide an unintended legacy for Greenwich. The small Old George tavern on the waterfront was renamed in its honour. No doubt its ale was enjoyed before and after this event by the hospital residents for it is only a few yards from the East Gate, located a short distance to the right of the Painted Hall and Chapel. The beautiful panelled rooms of the Trafalgar Tavern, designed in 1837 by architect Joseph Kay, would be named after the crew of *HMS Victory*. The balconies of the large refreshment area resemble the stern galley of his flagship; whitebait is usually served as a starter. The Liberal politicians once ate there. Charles Dickens would use the setting in his novel *Our Mutual Friend*. In 1996 it was voted the Evening Standard Pub of the Year.

Almost next door and adjoining the Curlew Rowing Club HQ is another old inn, The Yacht, once the Barley Mow. To the rear is Crane Street and a meander down will bring you to the Trinity Hospital almshouses, now under the Trusteeship of the Mercers Company. *Hospitale sanctae et individvae trinities grenwici* runs the inscription on the miniature crenellated façade, rebuilt in 1812. The tomb of the founder is inside, having been brought from Dover in 1696. Visiting is by appointment.

Continuing on a short distance along the Thames Path, beyond the generating station, brings you to a small backwater of pure delight; the quiet Georgian buildings of Ballast Quay where the gravel from Blackheath was loaded onto empty ships for stability. The solid square stone house used as the Harbour Master's Office is nearby. However, pride of place here must be the *Cutty Sark* tavern, a listed building circa 1695, plus a few renovations since. The period interior is decorated with illustrations of that unique class of vessel, the clipper. Outside, on the cobbled quay conveniently supplied with trestle tables, a close-up view can be obtained of the one million sq ft of

Teflon (90,000 Sq m) covering, tent-like, the Millennium Dome; the masts held up by 'forestays and backstays'. Apart from the name the tavern has no other connection with the vessel we see today in dry dock by Greenwich Pier.

Adjacent on Greenwich Peninsula, once a hive of industry, a flame still burns constantly on the former site of Europe's largest gasworks which closed in 1978 and now stores butane and naphtha feedstocks. Nearby is the old site of the Enderby Wharf, workplace in 1834 of three brothers who pioneered whaling in the Antarctic; honoured with an area named after them there before turning to the cable manufacture that would carry Greenwich Mean Time worldwide.

THE NATIONAL MARITIME MUSEUM

Officially opened on 27 April 1937 by George VI before an audience of 1,600 people – the first public engagement of his reign and three years after the Act of Parliament approving the museum's institution for the nation

The entrance to the stately, nautically-inspired facade is clearly signalled by two large buoys just inside the main entrance on Romney Road. If you glance obliquely to the left beyond the red buoy, Vanbrugh Castle is visible among the trees on the horizon. As we walk up the short pathway lined with anchors, discreet amplifiers relay the sound of the sea; waves cascading and swirling onto Chesil Beach in Dorset have been recorded. Before entering the main door, on your left you can see aloft through the ground-to-atrium window, a revolving crystal lantern; sparkling and marvellously crafted, from the former Tarbat Ness lighthouse on the Moray Firth in Scotland. To the right, similarly situated, is the giant burnished bronze frigate propeller Type 23 RN, also revolving, made by Stone Vickers of Erith, Kent. A few more steps and you are in rather a special place. The refurbished Neptune Court you have arrived in would perhaps please the old Roman sea god of that name, should he be around in spirit complete with dolphin and trident.

And warm the heart, too, of shipping magnate Sir James Caird, whose initial funding, equivalent to £100 million today, made possible the museum's very existence.

A canny Scot, he assiduously collected a vast personal collection of marine artefacts; many were obtained during the 1920s and '30s when available on the markets during the depression years. Passionately believing that the nation's maritime heritage should be preserved, he then donated them to enhance the nucleus of naval memorabilia and paintings originally housed in the Painted Hall of the Old Royal

Seamen's Hospital and later transferred to the Queen's House, adjacent to the Neptune Court building he financed. And while you get your bearings, you will not only hear the familiar intonations of the shipping forecast but you will also be entertained by a sixteen-minute film screening stretches of coastline, from Iceland to Scandinavia down through Europe to Spain and Portugal. The pictures of each location were taken by different photographers at the same time: 00.01 GMT on 12 December 1998.

There is discreet seating nearby, and throughout the museum. From this vantage point in the Neptune Court close to the shop and cloakrooms, you can also enjoy the delightfully gleaming, golden-cherub 'Sunbeam' figurehead and glimpse to the right the rotating engine from the paddle tug *Reliant*, that graced the Manchester Ship Canal for several decades. However you choose to voyage around, whether to 'swim, drift or paddle', you will also find yourself very challengingly 'on the ocean wave' of today and the future.

For the National Maritime Museum, originally opened to tell us the story of seafaring, has piloted itself splendidly with 'all sails unfurled' into the new century. The sixteen new galleries we see today superlatively enhance those already there, with many arranged around the East, South, and West Streets on the ground floor, Level 1. Here there are galleries dedicated to Explorers, Passengers, Rank and Style, Navigation and Maritime London, a Lecture Theatre and Submarine for Schools Area. The Library and Search Station are opposite the Hidden Treasures, by the exit to the colonnade connecting to the Queen's House. On Level 2, Trade and Empire, Art and the Sea and the Future of the Sea hold sway while Level 3 is now enhanced with the superb Oceans of Discovery Exhibition in the CP Ship's Gallery; the Friends' Grand Project requiring £300,000 in funding.

For of the total of some two million items held by the museum, thousands of amazing exhibits encompassing seafaring throughout the ages are on show for our enjoyment, examination, stimulation and education. If you can, allow for two hours inside. If you want to anchor awhile in the Neptune Court, refreshments can be enjoyed on Level 2 in the Upper Deck Coffee Bar. Here, your senses can also be effortlessly nourished to assimilate all that is around, above and below; enhanced in the clear airy spaciousness almost as though underwater itself. To the rear, courtesy of P&O, is The Bridge Gallery, evoking the excitement of the steering of ships for over a thousand years, from Viking long boats to Channel ferries. There is even more fun to be had in the adjacent All Hands Interactive Gallery, also exhibiting the marvellously executed teak model, in full sail, of *HMS Cornwallis*.

She was built in India in the late 18th century by the son of Master Shipbuilder Jamsetjee Bomanjee Wadia, using leftovers of the original materials. Although 1/16th of the total length of 170 ft (53 m), the model manages to fill a sizeable proportion of alcove space. The adjoining Ship of War Gallery has many other splendid models also on show.

Also from Level 2, below the largest unsupported atrium in Europe, you can easily view at leisure the varied technological, and other, displays surrounding you in cube and sphere; dedicated to the future of the sea which still carries 95% of global trade. On the 'horizon' the vast, windowed-stern of the 74-gun *HMS Implacable*, captured Hornblower-style from the French and renamed just a fortnight after fighting in the Battle of Trafalgar, hovers majestically; not over the sea in which she was scuttled almost in entirety off the Isle of Wight in 1949 – but simply onto the floor of Level 1. There her reprieved stern strikingly contrasts with an ornately gilded Royal Barge at her 'moorings'. Sixty-three feet long (20 m) and fantastically carved around 1732 by James Richards, successor to Grinling Gibbons, she was last used to row Queen Victoria's consort, Prince Albert, to open the new Coal Exchange in 1849! More illustriously, perhaps, on previous occasions Prince Frederick's barge glided on the Thames to the first public serenading of Handel's Water Music.

Almost alongside her golden bows and markedly emphasizing the product of a very different age rests the sleek, shiny, silvery hull, made from Alclad, of the 1930 vintage speedboat *Miss Britain III*. She was built by the British Power Boat Company in Southampton and designed by Hubert Scot-Paine; he would also develop early flying boats and fast gunboats for World War II. The surrounding 'streets' provide entrance to smaller galleries, coves of enchantment to be explored at will or whim. For what is a museum but a place where to ponder, meditate and muse? You can travel in spirit from Polynesia to the frozen wastes, share the privileges as first-class passengers on a transatlantic Cunard liner – and privations when steerage for a £6 one-way ticket.

You can enjoy the Planet Ocean Wave Tank, plumb the depths with divers and marvel in the compact and star-studded Navigation Gallery, dedicated by the Corporation of Trinity House. At the entrance, the words of John Masefield greet you: 'All I need is a Tall Ship and a Star to Steer Her By'. Stepping into the suitably darkened, circular 'Aladdin's cave' you are soon made subtly aware of the superbly-crafted contents within combining scientific skill and consummate artistry.

Immediately you cannot fail to see the hand-held model of the Global Positioning System (GPS) in use today; not unlike a domestic TV remote control unit and able to receive data from 27 satellites in low orbit. In stark contrast another exhibition case shows us an Arabic bronze astrolabe dated around 1250; much navigation then was safe only by adhering to established trade routes and always keeping sight of land.

We can trace, too, the developments of the backstaff, which attempted to define latitude by crudely measuring the angle between the sun and horizon with the observer standing behind the instrument; the quadrant came later around 1600.

The more accurate octant would be developed by John Hadley in 1731 and eventually the sextant; both would be used to measure the angles between the moon and the fixed stars.

Also on display are several globes. An intricately-designed, celestial, clockwork model, made by Isaac Habrecht circa 1646, could show the owner how to position mechanically in the northern hemisphere, simply by adjusting the globe to a specific latitude. Too late to aid Sir Francis Drake whose magnificent jewelled star brooch given to him by Queen Elizabeth I is exhibited along with a terrestrial globe dating from time of the Armada, eight years after his successful circumnavigation from 1577-80; the first to be attempted since the Portuguese expedition of Ferdinand Magellan in 1519 which returned with only 18 men out of the original complement of 260 and minus their leader.

Bur perhaps for sheer ingenuity and craftsmanship epitomising universal safety in seafaring go to Level 3 where, in the Oceans of Discovery Exhibition, possibly the pivot of the whole vast museum should deservedly rest on one small round object: the watch K1 with its clear white dial, taken on trial by Captain James Cook on his second expedition from 1772-75 in HMS Resolution and Adventure, and which finally solved the 'longitude problem'.

It is the first copy of the timepiece that proved to keep the absolutely essential accurate time at sea, after initial setting to Greenwich Mean Time: the revolutionary 5 inch diameter (12.5 cm) silver-encased precision watch. It was the first accurate sea-going clock ever and 'our never-failing friend' as Captain Cook reported to the Admiralty on his return. The neat winder and exquisitely-crafted interior are displayed alongside.

Also in this show case in the Age of Reason section of the Oceans of Discovery Exhibition can be found various other instruments essential to exploring and navigation including a marine barometer purchased from the sale of Mrs Cook's effect in 1835, a purposefully-made 24" Gregorian telescope such as her husband would have used for observing the transit of Venus and a sextant similar to one he would have used ashore to calculate longitude by the 'lunar distance method' in conjunction with reference to the Nautical Almanac. Thus, Captain James Cook repeatedly tested and confirmed the precision of K1.

Nearby a full-scale replica of the first sea-going clock of John 'Longitude' Harrison, the H1, can be observed busily in motion. This was made by Leonard Salzer of Biggin Hill, Kent, from 1970-76. The original H1 is in the Royal Observatory. Pride of place is also given to a 1:48 scale model of the Endeavour Bark, by Robert A Lightly of Capetown; dated 1975 and complete with ship's muster and stores. Another replica, installed ceremoniously via a window into this treasure trove of old and new amazing artefacts resulting from man opening up the world by sea down the centuries is the small lifeboat, the James Caird, built for the recent filming of 'Shackleton'.

Described as performing the longest rescue in history, the original James Caird was perilously navigated over 800 miles of freezing ocean by Ernest Shackleton from Elephant Island to South Georgia. A few years later, again in Antarctica, he died suddenly in 1922 and the sponsor of the expedition presented the boat to his old school, Dulwich College in south-east London. And if that other intrepid explorer of less icy waters, Francis Drake, who was obliged to steer the Golden Hinde with a pole attached to a rudder, ever wondered what became of the navy without him, he could rest assure that the majority of vessels appear to have been painted, drawn, modelled or photographed for display at the National Maritime Museum.

In contrast to these, the 'sound sculpture' of Bill Fontana's 'wave phases' in Dorset, plus other evocative and often vibrant tableaux and sculptures portray, in their own unique fashion, many other facets of life at sea.

There are fascinating figureheads aplenty, of all shapes, sizes and colours. The larger-than-life model from the *HMS Horatio* is suitably elevated by the entrance to the stimulating and very informative Nelson Gallery on Level 3. A majestic model from *HMS Thames* is proudly ensconced in the Maritime London Gallery, which is secreted behind a 'shop front' circa 1663 probably from, we are advised, Edward Lloyd's original coffee house in the City at Tower Street. Bridging a few centuries, a fibre optic glove with the potential to sense chemical agents and change colour according to temperature is set intriguingly in the floor in the nearby Rank and Style Gallery on Level 1. Up on Level 2, there is what might be considered, from a distance, to be a rather unconventional glass-and-steel, cable-crafted hammock slung near the stern of *HMS Implacable*. This, however, on closer inspection reveals itself as an innovative modern sculpture representation of *HMS Implacable*'s phantom hull, appropriately designated *Absentee*.

Since the spectres of the Roman galleys appeared in the English Channel, sea power has always been of immense concern to Julius Caesar's 'island colony'; the eventual Great Britain that grew into a maritime power and empire. That history is graphically recounted in the Wolfson Gallery of Trade and Empire, with the assistance of audio and visual technology. Also of interest in this gallery is the trio of large oil paintings reflecting the busy shipping commerce with China, including the late 18th century *European Factories in Canton* by William Daniell.

The superb expertise of the marine artists of several centuries is evident throughout the entire museum. Even before you reach the specifically designated Art and Sea Gallery, you cannot fail to notice the crisply-executed *Container Ships off Felixstowe* by John Wonnacott, 1994, on Level 1. Depending on which entrance you use to the Art and Sea Gallery, the refreshing *First of England* by the somewhat fittingly-named Humphrey Ocean, ingenuously depicting modern travel aboard a passenger ferry approaching Dover, is on hand to greet or bid you farewell.

Within the Art and Sea Gallery, a comprehensive selection of marine artistry is exhibited; relieved by a terracotta bust of Sir Walter Raleigh by Michael Rysbrack and a late 18th century decorated punchbowl destined for the export market of the Chinese Lung period circa 1785. An original copy of a photograph by David Hill and Robert Adamson, taken in 1844, reflects the lives of some inhabitants in the fishing village of Newhaven, near Edinburgh. Also compelling viewing are the authentic works in graphite, parchment, wash and oil on canvas by both the elder and young William Van der Veldes; they were brought over to England during the reign of Charles II and given a studio in the Queen's House in 1672.

The senior of the duo, we are told, was attributed the distinction of being the 'first official war correspondent', for he followed the naval fleets for over 20 years and painted in the midst of battles from a ketch; Charles II apparently put a stop to the practice, fearing mishaps. Following on after this illustrious pair and still with emphasis on safety at sea, it is interesting to note the contribution by the Friends of the painting by the splendidly-named Isaac Sailmaker of the *Second Eddystone Lighthouse*, around 1708.

A century and a half later James Whistler moved to Wapping, publishing his etchings in 1871. Today we can enjoy a few of these small gems; the *Thames Warehouse*, the *Black Lion Wharf*, the *Thames Police*, *The Pool* and *Limehouse* portraying life then in the East End. The residents, Whistler considered, were certainly as worthy of artistic record as those in the higher and more esteemed conditions of life, as was more customary. And of those below the waves, there are the revealing colour lithographs of the submarine prints by Eric Ravilious, an official War Artist lost at sea in 1942.

Elsewhere, as you wander around you may be able to identify in the NMM and the Queen's House William Dring's *Stand By Tubes* in the Control Room of *HMS Stubborn* and the silent eloquence of Barnett Friedman's ink and watercolour individual portraits of the 60 members of *HM Sub Tribune*'s company, during his sojourn aboard with them in 1943. The dignity and deceptive simplicity of Alan Durst's *Oak Bust of a Sailor*, pays tribute to the rank-and-file who gained no mention or special distinction in World War II; timelessly evocative of that dreadful period, the sculptor skilfully communicates the theme of 'anyman and everyman', as intended by the naval officer who commissioned the work.

The aerial assault on the already badly damaged German battleship,

Tirpitz, in the freezing fjords of Norway is interpreted on canvas by Charles Pears. The astounding 17 ft (5 m) long model, ratio 1:44, of the 35,000-ton battle ship King George V launched in 1935 gives considerable indication of the immensity of naval strength at 125,000 horsepower; in reality 745 ft (227 m) long. The shining bell of *HMS Valiant* mirrors the handwritten log of duty Midshipman Philip Mountbatten witnessing and recording the events off Cape Matopan in 1941. A copy of the Royal Navy Day by Day Book also furnishes a wealth of detail down the years of happenings in war and peace.

And when you have absorbed all you can manage there is always refreshment available in the Regatta Café on Level 2, also *al fresco* and exiting into Greenwich Park. A hundred or so yards to the right, by St Mary's Gate, you will find the delightful small Herb Garden and the granite statue of another midshipman, William IV, known as the Sailor King. On his death in 1837, he was succeeded by his niece, Victoria. She had celebrated her 18th birthday just a month earlier. In that same year, the physicist Charles Wheatstone and inventor William Fothergill Cooke took out the first British patent for the electric telegraph – another but then unbeknown 'giant step for mankind'. Greenwich Mean Time would soon be signalled across the oceans and the ships and seafarers of all nations would benefit forever.

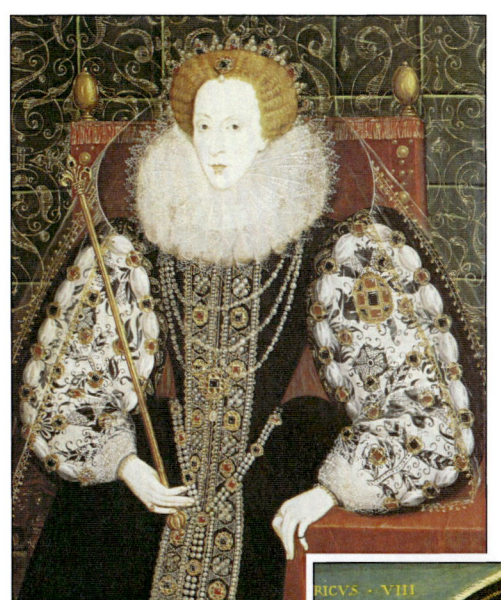

Elizabeth I
(National Maritime Museum)

Henry VIII
(National Maritime Museum)

Onion Dome: The Royal Observatory
(National Maritime Museum)

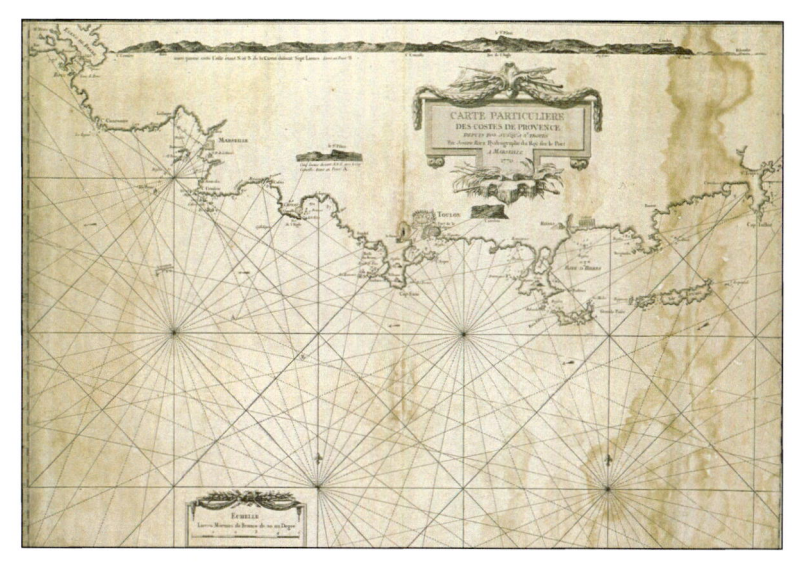

The Meridian Line: 0° Longitude
(National Maritime Museum)

The Octagon Room, The Royal Observatory
(National Maritime Museum)

The Dining Hall, Royal Naval College
(National Maritime Museum)

John Harrison's Clock 'H 4', which was to revolutionise navigation
(National Maritime Museum)

TIME OUT IN THE PARK WITH CAPTAIN COOK

"Not only as far as man has gone before, but as far as it is possible for man to go…"

A bronze statue of Captain James Cook, sculpted by Anthony Stones as recently as 1997, is soon to be positioned at the bottom of Jubilee Avenue, just south of the NMM and appropriately facing upwards to the Royal Observatory on the horizon.

A prestigious setting for a superb navigator and esteemed mariner, born at Marton-le-Cleveland, Yorkshire, in 1728 and educated at the village school in Great Ayton; the fees paid by the farmer who employed his father as foreman. Apprenticeship followed, when aged seventeen, to the grocery and haberdashery store at Staithes in the North Riding. Within a year this was transferred, presumably at his request, to the coalship owner and Quaker, Captain John Walker, living at Grape Lane in Whitby. The house, close to the harbour and not far from the yards near the River Esk where the colliers, or Whitby 'cats', were built, is now a museum dedicated to the achievements of this remarkable apprentice.

The names of the *Endeavour, Resolution, Adventure* and *Discovery*, all built at Whitby, have passed into history. The loss of the youthful James Cook's expertise in drapery and acumen in the village stores would eventually become the seafarer's gain. Captain Walker soon realised the potential of the newest addition to his family of apprentices. They lodged in the attic of his home and learned their trade on the coalships plying the coast between Newcastle and London, then considered 'The best nursery of seamen'.

When not at sea, the young James Cook was set to work on navigation and mathematics during the long winter evenings; a far cry from the braids and buckles of his first venture into employment, but perhaps of interest to him later. It was during this time, around 1748, that the Royal Navy first introduced uniform; the monarch, George II, having been apparently greatly impressed by the navy and gold riding habit of the Duchess of Bedford.

And no doubt, the once very eager student of seafaring would be gratified to know that not only are his sextant and the first marine chronometer ever used, K1, displayed at the National Maritime Museum, which evolved from a small collection in the Old Royal Seamen's Hospital where he was given an honorary appointment, but that the Draper's Company would one day sponsor a gallery within the museum. In the Rank and Style Gallery, varieties of naval dress are closeted in cubicles and their details are helpfully explained with the aid of audio. And probably unthinkable to Captain Cook, the uniform of WRNS included.

From where his statue now stands at Greenwich, it is not so very far to his home in the Mile End Road in south-east London where he once lived. More central, however, is his other memorial in The Mall, near Admiralty Arch.

For it was as Able Seaman James Cook that he joined the Royal Navy in 1755. After his apprenticeship, he had served two years 'before the mast' in the Baltic Trade. Returning to Whitby in 1752, he further honed his skills as Mate on the colliers off the east coast for three years. The turning point came in 1755 when, with the possibility of war with France looming, he refused the offer of a command from Captain Walker and enlisted. They would remain lifelong friends. Within a month of joining the Royal Navy, he was promoted to Master's Mate. Three years later he would navigate and chart the St Lawrence River, prior to the naval assault on Quebec. After a few years, his expertise in mathematics, astronomy and marine surveying resulted in his appointment to the Newfoundland Survey; his charting would eventually be published in the *North American Pilot*.

During this period he also recorded his *Observations and*

Calculation of the Longitude therefrom of an eclipse of the sun in the Burgeo Islands in 1766. The following year it would be published in the *Royal Society Philosophical Transactions*, receiving the praise that "The observer was a good mathematician and very expert in his business…"

It is not therefore surprising that Lieutenant James Cook was commissioned in 1768 to command *HMS Endeavour Bark*, an upgraded Whitby collier bought by the Admiralty to take observers to Tahiti to witness the transit of Venus for the Royal Society. Britain was taking part in an international scientific effort to calculate the distance of the Earth from the sun. After leaving Tahiti, his orders were to sail south and resume geographical discovery in the search for further continental land.

With the blessing of George III, the 121 ft long (32 m) vessel, with 90 crew, sailed from Plymouth. This was the first Royal Naval expedition to officially combine scientific objectives. Sharing the journey, and Great Cabin with some of their specimens, was a young Joseph Banks who would later help found the Royal Botanic Gardens at Kew and his Swedish botanist friend, Daniel Solander. Unfortunately, although the necessary observations of Venus were made, the calculations fluctuated so erratically that the astronomical results were inconclusive; this was due to the condition of the planet itself. Also, unable to find the elusive southern continent, the intrepid commander then set course for New Zealand as instructed, all the while expertly surveying and charting.

With *HMS Endeavour* on course for home via the unknown eastern side of Australia, which was also successfully charted, the heavily-laden vessel ran aground on the Great Barrier Reef on two occasions in 1770. Cook was then obliged to jettison some four-pound guns and their carriages, each weighing 1000 pounds (450 Kg) in order to refloat. Almost exactly two hundred years later, in 1969, six of these would be found encased in living coral just over 4 ft thick (1 m); one, now bereft of encrustation, has pride of place outside the entrance to the

Navigation Gallery. It might be reasonable to assume that had Cook been able to access Greenwich Mean Time with a sea-going clock, enabling him to calculate the longitude of his position with extreme exactitude, these regrettable incidents might not have occurred.

As it was, he could only refer to the newly published *Nautical Almanac* recording the exact angle between the moon and certain fixed stars measured at three-hourly intervals, and thus arrive at Greenwich Mean Time. Although reliable, it was a slow and complicated method to calculate longitude by comparing the assessment of the local time with Greenwich Mean Time. The deductions could take several hours. However, he returned home safely in 1771 and was promoted commander. That his voyage was a success, navigationally, is beyond doubt.

When Captain Cook sailed the oceans there was still no fixed point of 0.00 degrees longitude, internationally recognised, for mariners. He has been famously painted surrounded by many charts; it is not hard to understand why. Audio communication to ships at sea was impossible. The signalling of GMT at the entrance to ports by time balls and guns had yet to be devised. Even a few degrees off course at sea then could be disastrous when out of sight of land, unless you could accurately calculate from your last position – or somewhere – the length of time you had sailed as the Earth rotated simultaneously at a rate of one degree every four minutes; after making allowance for speed and course, you could determine exactly where you were. That elusive *somewhere* would one day be at Greenwich, in the cool climes of south-east England.

James Cook embarked on his second voyage in 1772, taking on trial for the Admiralty the small precision watch K1. The epic voyage in *HMS Resolution* and *HMS Adventure* would take him to the Arctic, Antarctica and much of the Tropics, including Easter Island and Tonga. Bases in New Zealand and Tahiti were used for replenishment. On his return he would report to the Secretary of the Admiralty that the trial "Exceeded the expectations of its most zealous advocate and was a faithful guide, through all vicissitudes of climate, the watch did not deceive us". For en voyage, with his 'trusty friend, the watch' he had been able to work out positions to within 2 miles (3 Km), correlating his deductions with the *Nautical Almanac* for proof.

It is highly probable that without K1 he might not have been able to achieve, during his second voyage that lasted from 1772-5, three visits to the Antarctic, discover and chart South Georgia and the neighbouring uninhabited South Sandwich Islands.

He returned home, having reached and charted a southerly latitude of 71 degrees and 10 minutes, and a longitude calculated at 106 degrees and 54 minutes. The Royal Society, elected him a member and also issued a coveted Copley Medal for his paper on scurvy; the disease being almost as much a menace at sea as lack of longitude. It would not be until 1795, however, that the regular administration of lemon juice became *de rigeur* in the Royal Navy, but was changed to lime juice in 1865, possibly for reasons of economy. This regime was then adopted by the Merchant Navy. Although the shelf-life of limes was found to be less than that of lemons, these routines proved very efficacious. The length of voyages shortened as steamships prevailed, by then the globe was charted and safety at sea much improved. The British sailors, however, became known as 'limeys'.

It has been suggested that Captain Cook's second voyage is possibly the most informative sea voyage ever undertaken; and that the completed trio are on par with the space exploration of the 20th century. Their details and hazards have been well documented; the first voyage alone records significant mortality among the ship's company when his usually healthy crew succumbed to dysentery and malaria when passing through Batavia on their way home. And as we know, Captain Cook himself did not return from the third voyage; receiving a fatal wound during a minor scuffle in 1779 when putting back to shore at Keala Kekua in Hawaii. A repair was found necessary to a sprung topmast soon after leaving harbour; his swift return was misinterpreted as of hostile intent by a few inhabitants.

By then, however, having been at sea since June 1776 in the *Resolution* and *Discovery*, he had voyaged to New Zealand and discovered Hawaii which he charted as the Sandwich Islands; they would be annexed by the United States in 1898 and a naval base established at Pearl Harbour. Captain Cook then worked his way up the Pacific coastline of North America to the Bering Strait, until prevented by pack ice from going further. It had been his intention to try to discover a north-west passage. He fatefully returned to Hawaii for the winter and was succeeded by Captain Charles Clerke, previously in command of *Discovery*, but sadly he died of consumption after another attempt at the Bering Strait. It is recorded that the ships returned home eventually to England in October 1780 under the command of one John Gore.

Captain James Cook was greatly esteemed by his peers and had much respect for others. He was revered also for his excellent planning and administration, as well as his ability to handle men; maybe his year of weighing out the flour and sorting out sizes of buttons, as demanded by the general public in the village shop, had been fruitful in other ways. He would no doubt applaud the situating of the Prime Meridian of the World at the Royal Observatory Greenwich; built on what is affectionately and colloquially known as 'Clock Hill'.

THE QUEEN'S HOUSE

"…So finished and furnished, that it far surpasseth all other of that kind in England."

(Comment by visitor during reign of Charles I.)

Today we can quite simply go inside the Queen's House and see the same view as Charles I and that of his son Charles II who, so history relates, looked up the hill one day from the balcony and saw the place to build the Royal Observatory.

The entrance leads from the park into the brick-vaulted undercroft. A bust of Inigo Jones immediately greets you; sculpted by the Antwerp-born John Michael Rysbrack, working in marble and not his frequent terracotta. The Queen's House was very much Inigo Jones' brainchild. It was thought something of a novelty when first assembled, and described as 'a curious device costing 4000li'. Initially there was only one storey in an 'H' shape, with a bridge on the first floor level straddling the noisy and dirty Deptford to Woolwich stretch of the London to Dover road.

During refurbishment in the 1930s this disused road was temporarily re-opened from the basement area; photographs of that time are now displayed on the ground floor in the Historic Greenwich Gallery, with a topographical model of the Greenwich site on the scale of 1:1000, as it was in 1638. The most recent refurbishment took place for the Millennium and the Queen's House was redesignated as the museum's Art Centre. This decision allowed more of the vast archives to see the light of day; all available space is now utilised as a major exhibition and education area.

On ground level, it is the sublime proportions of the Great Hall that remind you vividly for what purpose the house was devised and built, primarily that of entertainment. The black and white marble floor was laid in 1636-7, some two decades after the building began, by Charles

I's Master Mason, Nicholas Stone. The cantilevered-in-oak minstrels' gallery and pine-beamed ceiling complements the design of the floor; shown off to discrete perfection by the white and matt 'old gold' finish of the original decoration. It is pleasantly empty, light and airy.

The only other decorative evidence of 'times past' in the Great Hall now are the portraits of 'The Admiral's Men' painted for Queen Anne by the German artist Godfrey Kneller and Michael Dahl of Sweden; they adorn the minstrels' gallery which leads into the first-floor art exhibition rooms. The spaciousness on the ground floor is relieved only by the four marble busts of senior British admirals; these were commissioned by the Royal Naval School when moving into the Queen's House in 1807 and sculpted by Francis Chantrey, the son of a Yorkshire carpenter who would also train as a portrait painter.

Nowadays, entertainment is now very much 'back on the menu' at the Queen's House. Performances by professional actors relate lively accounts of other eras, in period costumes, in the Great Hall. There are also music sessions, both instrumental and vocal.

Near the ground floor entrance is a picture gallery devoted to the 'Tudors of Greenwich' containing superb portraits of that period; plus a very large oil painting of the Somerset House Conference of 1604, convened a year after the death of the last of the Tudors, Queen Elizabeth I. Brilliantly executed by Juan Pantoja de la Cruz, the eleven delegates are assembled at a long table to sort out a peace treaty between England and Spain, some sixteen years after the Armada. No doubt they would be interested to know that just a few hundred yards away on Romney Road, a conference centre and hotel now exist on the Greenwich World Heritage Site.

Another possible function of the Queen's House was that it was perhaps intended to serve as a reception base and temporary residence for visiting royalty and diplomats arriving in London by sea. And perhaps useful as a grandstand for hunting and military parades, not to mention keeping dry the feet of the royal residents when they left the palace on the riverfront and crossed into Greenwich Park! The road, which was later moved to become the present Romney Road, was known to be notoriously muddy and it was around here that Sir Walter Raleigh reputedly laid his cloak for Elizabeth I in a 'plashy place'. The queen consort of her successor, James VI of Scotland, the extravagant Anne of Denmark commissioned Inigo Jones to build for her the Queen's House, as it became known, on the site of the gateway to the rear of Elizabeth's Tudor palace, close to where Henry VIII and his magnificent court, had jousted and revelled. Recent excavations denoted the exact locations.

Jones based his design on a villa built for the Medici Dynasty in 1485 just outside Florence, at Poggio a Caiano, by Guiliano de Sangallo; a member of a renowned family of Italian Renaissance architects and military engineers. The white-cemented exterior, tall windows and Ionic columns were then unique in England; Inigo Jones somewhat 'went to town' with his innovative idea for, what might be thought, a gigantic summerhouse at the end of the garden of the royal palace. Nothing like it had certainly ever been seen before. The building was known sometimes as The White House and apart from also being referred to, perhaps derogatorily, as 'the dancing barne' for the court of James I, no other official name was ever given apart from the one we know today.

Although only one masque was held there during James I's reign, it is considered that the house was primarily intended for that purpose by the entertainment-loving Scandinavian-born Queen; too poor to have a marriage dowry. The Islands of Orkney and Shetland were ceded to Scotland instead.

Since the time of Henry VIII and his flamboyant court, the participants and audiences of the dancing masques understood only too well the technical brilliance and symbolism of these events; the sophisticated choreography held much hidden meaning perhaps including that of menace. The dramatist, Ben Jonson, would supply the text for many of Inigo Jones' colourful masterpieces, sometime using innovative 'moving' scenery.

James I loved rich garments himself and established silk mills at nearby Lewisham, possibly to supply himself and his many favourites at court. The Silk Mill Path is still there, by the railway arches, running alongside the riverbank parallel to the lower ground floor of Tesco. Greenwich Park continued to be very popular for James I loved riding, his legs having been weakened during a sickly childhood; he excelled at hunting so near to London when he could tear himself away from Whitehall.

Greenwich House was very much the domain of Queen Anne, who died in 1619, only three years after the Queen's House was begun. Such was the cost of the court there was hardly enough money 'in the coffers' for her funeral; it is on record that she lay unburied for many weeks. By then only the first floor of the Queen's House had been completed. An economic tarpaulin of thatch was put in place overhead and the building was left for a decade. Her son, Charles I, in turn would 'give' Greenwich to his wife, Henrietta Maria, who asked Inigo Jones to continue with his grand design. By 1638 there was a Central Bridge Room and loggia on the first floor, the Great Hall had two storeys and a gallery for minstrels. Most of the carving of the interior was completed; it was also sumptuously decorated and furnished throughout.

The amazing 'tulip' stairs still concertina steadily upward into space from the ground floor; originally leading to a polygonal turret on the roof. They were always an integral part of Inigo Jones' initial design; their name is derived from the recurrent pattern of a flower motif, supposedly tulip, on the wrought-iron balustrade. The construction was, we are told, the first centrally unsupported spiral stair in Britain, completed in about 1635 at the height of the European 'Tulip Phase'; a period which brought financial disaster to many on the Continent but has left us a beautiful legacy of intricate workmanship and design.

For Henrietta Maria it was her 'House of Delights'; and also a powerful showcase of state wealth to impress visiting dignitaries. It was used frequently until 1642 when the political and religious strife erupted in Civil War. She would not return for 20 years – and her husband never. Eventually tried for treason, on the bleak winter morning of 30 January 1649 Charles I would step through the window of Inigo Jones' Banqueting House at Whitehall onto a scaffold. In so doing, the absolute rule of monarchy disappeared forever in England. The executioner's fee was £30, Windsor the final resting place.

There was considerable destruction at the Greenwich royal complex during Oliver Cromwell's 'Commonwealth'; in 1652, the state apartments were demoted to stables and there were various other unfortunate uses. Dutch prisoners of war were also detained on the site. Oliver Cromwell, however, liked the Queen's House, as he did Ely Cathedral, and this probably also saved it from devastation by his soldiers. It would be used as a Roundhead headquarters, but he did not live there, preferring Hampton Court and the surrounding countryside. Many of the paintings, sculptures and other precious items were removed and dispersed, also never to return.

Meanwhile, the brilliant designer of the luxurious fashions for the court masques, Inigo Jones, had taken refuge at Basing House in Hampshire. He was obliged by the Roundheads to flee one night, clad ignominiously only in a blanket. His estate was confiscated, but later restored. He died in 1652, aged 79, mourning his monarch to the end.

When Charles II was restored to the monarchy in 1660, building at Greenwich resumed; the remainder of the old Tudor palace was demolished for safety reasons. The Queen's House was extended to a 'square' with two additional bridge rooms, as we see it today; the cost of refurbishment then being some £75,000. The overgrown and neglected Greenwich Park was landscaped from 1661 until 1663, when the money ran out; the architect and mathematician Andre Le Notre had worked at Versailles for Louis IV and Saint Cloud for Charles II's sister, the Duchess of Orleans.

Whether Andre Le Notre visited personally is uncertain. It has been suggested that the avenue of chestnut trees alongside the Royal

Observatory, then Greenwich Castle, should have continued down to the Queen's House; he may have been unaware that Greenwich Park sloped so much. However, the plans were certainly adhered to by Henry Jermyn, Earl of St Albans, High Steward and Lord Chamberlain. A great admirer of Inigo Jones, he would have much influence on the subsequent development of the influence of classical architecture at Greenwich from 1660-76.

Henry Jermyn was a close personal friend of Queen Henrietta Maria, who died at Colombes near Paris in 1669, some twenty years after her husband's execution.

After her son's restoration she returned to Greenwich for a short while, but was never happy in England again and returned to her homeland. Henrietta Maria's gay light heartedness, love of dancing and wont of personally participating in masques had annoyed the Puritans. Some of the blame for the outbreak of the Civil War would forever be laid at her feet. A reputedly devoted wife and concerned mother who sold her jewels to fund the Royalist cause; nevertheless, perhaps not astute enough to be her husband's best political adviser.

The monarchy gradually transferred permanently 'up west'. The Deptford to Woolwich Road was moved northwards a short distance to become the present Romney Road, in 1699. The Queen's House remained Crown property. Its subsequent history would be somewhat chequered and included being occupied by the Ranger of Greenwich Park. One incumbent of that honorary post, Sarah, Duchess of Marlborough, during her sojourn from 1702-14 managed to transfer the ceiling panels from the cubic Great Hall to her new London home; the present Marlborough House in The Mall – they are still there. Procuring the paintings was insufficient; they were 'cut down to size' as well. Other occupants of the Queen's House would be the Governors of the Royal Seamen's Hospital and later the boys and girls of the Royal Naval School; orphans and children of officers and seamen. The colonnades were begun around 1806, a memorial to Nelson and following the route of the old Deptford to Woolwich

Road. The architect was Daniel Asher Alexander, also responsible for Dartmoor Prison.

The Royal Hospital School was Britain's largest school of navigation and known we are told, as 'the cradle of the navy' The entrance age was 5-12 years; the dormitories were 50-bedded. The diet seems to have been mainly bread and butter, beef and cocoa; a preparation perhaps for the bully beef and ship's biscuit of the future.

The Lower School taught boys to be seamen and the girls were trained for domestic service. The Upper School taught navigation. A training ship with safety nets around the hull was 'berthed' in front of the Queen's House.

Apparently the 'closeness of the sexes led to many evils' and the 300 girls moved out in 1841; the 700 boys left in 1933 for Holbrook, near Ipswich in Suffolk. It remains there, having reverted to co-education, still run by Greenwich Hospital for the support of seafarers and their families. Now a major independent boarding school of academic repute it has 680 full-time boarders aged 11-18 years; assistance may be given with fees.

It is interesting to note that a rather weather-beaten plaque can be found located on the side wall of the NMM, to the left of the main entrance and facing the colonnade.

This commemorates former pupils who chose to have their ashes scattered on the lawns around the Queen's House. Obviously they had happy memories of their school days at Greenwich, despite the 5 am rising bell.

The Queen's House was then extensively restored after over a century of institutional wear and tear and became the centre of the new National Maritime Museum. There was a 'Stuart Restoration Period' from 1984-99 when it was refurbished to some of the former glory of Charles II and Catherine of Braganza; the furnishings reflecting the opulence and magnificence of their apparent lifestyle are now removed

But still there for our delight are the original ceiling beams in the

Great Hall and the cornices and friezes of the King's Presence Chamber; executed in pine by Thomas James and Richard Dirgin who worked at the Queen's House under the direction of Inigo Jones. The illustrious pair, however, were also much desired by the Royal Navy to use their skills on Charles I's theatrically decorated *Sovereign of the Seas*, then being built at nearby Woolwich at a cost of £65,586. Peter Lely's portrait of this gigantic ship, with Shipwright Peter Pett, is in the King's Anteroom; Godfrey Kneller's *Samuel Pepys* hangs over the modern chimney-piece which is based on an original Inigo Jones sketch of 1637.

The King's Side Closet has the original 1630s chimney surround. The adjacent King's Closet is now an Oil Painting Conservation Studio, complete with illuminated screen showing some of the treatments being carried out on the canvases, staffed by a series of Artists in Residence. The King's Presence Chamber is also devoted to the works of Van Dyck, who succeeded Daniel Mytens at the court of Charles I. The arch foe, Oliver Cromwell, is depicted in a terracotta bust by Rysbrack.

The King's and Queen's Bedchambers both have the original coved ceilings of 1660; the East Bridge Room has the fine fret ceiling done by Charles II's expert Master Plasterer, John Grove. This style of plasterwork would find much favour in great houses throughout England during the 18th and 19th centuries. The Queen's Presence Chamber retains the ornate, coved and what is officially described as 'grotesquely painted' plaster ceiling panels attributed to Matthew Gooderich or possibly John de Gritz, around the 1630s. The chimney-piece is a resin cast of the original and probably styled by Inigo Jones.

A double long case clock by Daniel Quare, circa 1710, is in the King's Bedchamber. He made clocks for William III, Queen Mary and Queen Anne; this model shows sidereal time – calculated by the stars – Greenwich Mean Time, the day, month and 'Equation of Time'. There is also a slightly earlier astronomical clock, circa 1705, by

Edward Cockey of Warminster, below the South Stairs; this shows the times of sunrise and sunset throughout the year.

Small wonder with such a history that the Queen's House has a reputation for being haunted; this has been seriously documented.

TIME OUT ON ONE TREE HILL WITH THE TUDORS

"Here fair Eliza, Virgin Queen,
From business free, enjoyed the scene
Here oft in pensive mood she stood
And kindly plan'd for Britain's good
So record tells and this beside
Sang ditties to the silver tide
Full worth such honours are thou still
Belov'd of thousands, One Tree Hill"

(*London Chronicle*, May 25-27, 1784)

A short distance from The Pond by Park Row Gate and up a moderate slope, this verse can be found inscribed on the bench beneath a plane tree; dedicated to a monarch declared illegitimate when three years old, imprisoned in the Tower of London and tried for treason when aged twenty-one only to be crowned Queen four years later and herald in the never-to-be-forgotten Elizabethan era.

Looking across the Thames now, Elizabeth I would see the Canary Wharf business complex, valued at billions, on the Isle of Dogs; once a marsh where her father kept hunting packs. Below, she would not recognise where she was born four centuries ago in September 1553 at the rambling Tudor riverside 'Palace of Placentia'. There, in 'the pleasant place' as a young princess she had shared some of her life with her step-siblings; the future Catholic Queen Mary I, who would later send her to the Tower for supposed involvement in Protestant plots, and sickly brother, Edward VI. His teenage death at Greenwich after various traumatic treatments for consumption is luridly recorded.

Growing into womanhood she had skilfully danced at the revelries and coped with her various stepmothers, all the while acutely absorbing political intrigue. For when not secluded in country houses, it was at the Palaces of Greenwich, Whitehall and Hampton Court that she could show her brilliance at French, Italian and the Classics; as well as indulging in swearing and the boxing of ears when the occasion demanded and she thought fit. A good preparation, we might conclude, for someone who would see the beacon lit on nearby Shooter's Hill to announce the sighting of the Armada in 1588, sign the orders at Greenwich for repelling the invasion from Spain and then inspire 2000 of her troops downriver at Tilbury; flashing a silver breastplate and gowned in white with matching gelding, all the while eloquently ad libbing.

England would be spared. No doubt today Elizabeth I would gasp with pride at what she would see around her, pleased that the site is now used mainly for educational purposes. We are told that she liked to visit the laboratories of the scientists of her day on Thameside and was shown by Sir Walter Raleigh how to 'weigh smoke'. Upriver at Deptford, her grandfather Henry VII, who was much concerned with trade, encouraged shipbuilding, adroitly convened a navigational act to ensure only English ships carried English goods and built the first Royal dockyard at Portsmouth in 1496. He had previously disposed of Richard III at Bosworth Field in 1485 and consummated the event even more adroitly by marrying his dead enemy's niece, Elizabeth of York; so ending the distinctly non-fragrant Wars of the Roses and uniting the House of Lancaster forever with their former foes. He then proceeded to rebuild at Greenwich.

His son, Henry VIII, would inherit an improved and more regal palace on the riverside. An absolute monarch and always larger than life, not content with merchant ships armed with guns for protection of his realm, he pioneered the building of 'battle ships'. for his quarrel with the Pope made him fearful of war. He thus began the Royal Dockyard at Woolwich downriver for the creation of his flagship. It was easier to equip and man his ships from London; the Tower stocked munitions. *Henry Grace a Dieu* otherwise *The Great Harry* would be the largest warship of its day but unfortunately burned down in 1533. Woolwich would later become renowned for the Royal Arsenal and other military establishments; much of the fine architecture remains. The Brass Foundry at Woolwich was built in 1717 and is the oldest building still in use. It has been a museum since 1974 and now houses archives of the NMM.

Henry VIII also extended the shipbuilding facilities upriver at Deptford; around 1512-13 founding the Royal Naval Dockyard, the King's Yard. The Victualling Board would be based there and down the years given the unappetising accolade of 'Old Weevil'; despite a visit by Queen Victoria granting royal status and the emergence of the first factory assembly line in the world for manufacturing biscuits. In more recent times the site would be used as a cattle-market. The tidal Thames silted up and large scale shipbuilding was transferred to the Royal Docks created at Chatham and Plymouth.

However, Elizabeth I might be interested to know, like us, that some of the buildings in the King's Yard at Deptford survive to this day. One that we can visit is the Master Shipwright's House. Rebuilt once in 1708 when severely dilapidated, recent intervention is providing further refurbishment and upgrading to the Shipwright's Palace Museum (see Tips for Tourists).

And if Elizabeth I looked across a short distance from One Tree Hill today she would see another museum, but nearer home and straddling the horizon; the quasi-Jacobean redbrick Flamsteed House and the domed edifices of the Meridian Building and Planetarium comprising the Royal Observatory Greenwich we know today. She would have known the site when built on as a hunting lodge by her father and for possibly imprisoning her mother, Anne Boleyn, for a brief period when en route to the Tower of London for trial and subsequent execution; her alleged misdemeanours being portrayed as both very shocking and numerous.

But perhaps Elizabeth I would be as refreshed as most of us visiting today to see the simple orange aluminium Time Ball, on the top of Flamsteed House, which would give such help to seafarers from the early 19th century onwards. She was only too well aware of the dangers at sea for mariners, when relying only on latitude for correct positioning of their vessels. The first Englishman to successfully circumnavigate the globe, Francis Drake, spent many hours relating his experiences to her. A remarkable feat for sailors then in the late 16th century, often hampered by squalls and the rolling of the ship, using only the rudimentary cross-staff, designed for use on land as a portable sundial for 'telling the time'. By measuring the length of the sun's shadow at midday from a scale along the base a position north and south of the equator could be crudely estimated – and thus the distance travelled. But when navigating at sea, measuring the length of the shadow of the sun at midday was almost impossible and very unreliable. It was far easier to measure the angle of the sun on the horizon at midday when it was nearest, and compare the reading with that of a known position on land, often the home port.

The invention of the backstaff by Captain John Davis, the Devon-born prolific Tudor mariner and expert navigator, would be invaluable. This lined up the shadow of the sun with a view of the horizon through an eyepiece, giving a more accurate reading; when checked against a table of predicted angles a latitude north or south of the equator could be calculated. He upgraded this with the 'Davis Double Quadrant', plus a handbook on practical navigation, *The Seaman's Secrets*, in 1594 towards the end of Elizabeth's reign. An ardent and optimistic believer in the possibility of the existence of a north-west passage through the Canadian arctic to the Orient, John Davis also published *The World's Hydrographical Description* a year later. His experiences with the intense reflection of the arctic icefields had inspired him to revise the cross-staff so that it could be used facing away from the sun; hence the 'backstaff'. Thus, the Tudor mariners navigated by day from the nearest star to Earth, the sun, or at night by the height of the exceedingly luminous and nearly always constant Pole Star (the lodestar) in the northern hemisphere, and the Southern Cross below the equator.

The local time, when it could be estimated from the nearest

sundial, varied all over the world as they sailed. But there was no way of accurately correlating the *meri dies* or 'middle of the day' reading of the sun with the actual time aboard ship. By calculating one degree north/south to equal the length of one degree of latitude, they could establish their position in relation to the 0.00 degree of the equator. Going east-west-east was the problem; sailing horizontally on the Earth's surface with its almost vertical axis rotating full-circle every twenty-four hours.

Travelling along routes described in the chart-books of sailing directions and anchorages, the invaluable *portolanos* known to the Greeks and Romans, the Tudor mariners followed 'rhumb-lines' drawn as extensions and measured in leagues (3 miles/5 Km) from compass points on land. They used the natural ore of lodestone, magnetite (the magnetic oxide of iron), rubbed over their wooden compass needles; steel instruments had yet to be perfected. Provided there were not too many strong currents or cross winds, they relied on 'dead reckoning' by guessing their location; setting the speed of their vessels against the angle of the prevailing winds.

The speed of a ship was calculated in 'knots', using for time-measurement a sand glass, turned every 28 seconds. Simultaneously, the sailors counted the knots, tied at approximately 50 ft intervals (15m), on a line thrown into the sea. This was attached to a triangle of wood known as the 'log'. The knot would become the unit of speed equivalent to a 'nautical mile per hour' (1.15 miles per hour); always longer than a land mile for it is the length of the Earth's surface measured along an arc, not as a straight line. Hourly the sailors on watch entered their observations of speed, courses and distances covered, using K for knots and HK for fractions, in their log books and sometimes adding 'doodling' to their accomplishments as they eked out long hours aboard. In 1730 the Admiralty made log-keeping compulsory; these were to be handed in at 6-monthly intervals.

Many 'logs' are now in the vast archives of the National Maritime Museum; recognised as a very valuable source of information relating to climatic changes and the Earth's magnetic fields, with particular relevance for reference today with regard to global warming; intensive studies of 'times past' may yield important clues for future trends. The Library and Hydrographic Collections in the National Maritime Museum contain over 80,000 maps and charts covering most areas of the world and dating from the 15th century. There are over 1000 printed atlases also from that time; many examples produced by famous cartographers, including Ptolemy.

The *portulanos* range from a survey of the north-east Atlantic Ocean and Mediterranean Sea, drawn by Bertran and Ripol in 1456, to a chart of the east coast of North America by Southake and Fitzhugh, dated 1693; ten years before the death of Elizabeth I. During her lifetime, the development of the small clock or watch had also begun. In 1542, when she was nine years old, Peter Henlein died. He was born in Nuremburg at the end of the previous century and pioneered the 'mainspring', as the energy store in place of the earlier falling-weight. This could be conveniently used in a small clock capable of being worn on a person. At first, these were very bulky, often cylindrical and usually worn round the waist on a girdle; a belt often made of cord. Around 1680, Robert Hooke, an esteemed instrument-maker and Professor of Geometry at Gresham College in London, who advised Christopher Wren with the design of the Royal Observatory, perfected the 'hairspring' watch; a feat also claimed by Christiaan Huygens in Holland. Possibly, along with many other inventions and discoveries around this time, some 'great minds thought alike', wherever they were.

But two great minds that did not think alike in order to reach their same objective, the calculation of longitude, were the uncompromising and unyielding in their quests for perfection, John Flamsteed and John Harrison. Each ploughed their own lonely furrow. Neither would suffer fools gladly.

The Royal Observatory was opened just seventy years after the end of the Tudor dynasty. No doubt Elizabeth I and Sir Francis Drake would be proud to know that in a place they knew so well, the calculation of the 'apparent solar time' when affected by the varying speed of the Earth orbiting around the sun combined with the tilt of its axis, would result in a 'mean time' based at Greenwich, used worldwide as clock time. Just inside the entrance of the Royal Observatory, you will be greeted today with the GMT Accurist Clock; accurate to 1/10 of a second by the atomic time signals broadcast 'round-the-clock' from the BT Radio Station, near Rugby in Warwickshire; the county where Elizabeth I gave Kenilworth Castle to her long-time favourite, Lord Robert Dudley.

Another Warwickshire resident and contemporary, William Shakespeare, was born in the market town of Stratford upon Avon. In the autumn of 1599 he would open his beloved Globe Theatre on the bawdy side of the Thames at Bankside. Oliver Cromwell had been born that spring; during the Civil War four decades later it would be closed and fall into ruin. Writing in *As You Like It* Shakespeare referred to a pocket sundial simply as 'a dial from a poke'. We may well wonder with what eloquent prose he would describe a modern radio-controlled wrist watch automatically programmed to Greenwich Mean Time and British Summer Time. A score of artificial moons each with several atomic clocks now orbit 10,000 miles (16,000 Km) above the globe on the US Global Positioning Satellite (GPS), relaying latitude and longitude precisely to hand-held receivers, perhaps to be complemented by the £2 billion European Galileo Project.

THE ROYAL OBSERVATORY GREENWICH
HOW AND WHEN – NOW AND THEN

"We have resolved to build a small observatory within our park and at Greenwich, upon the highest ground…"

(Royal Warrant, 22 June 1675.)

The exiled Stuart, Charles II, sailed home in 1660 to a restored but fragile and flamboyant throne which had survived a republic of eleven years, from Renaissance Holland; a country with a profound interest in the study of light reflected by the invention of superb scientific instruments. The philosophy of observation, coupled with intensity of looking, was becoming an intellectual 'timebomb' throughout Europe and Charles II was greatly interested in science. As monarch of an expanding maritime trading nation whose ships were in danger from hostile enemy fleets foraging the oceans, he was only too well aware of the necessity for accurately calculating time at sea.

During the ensuing years, the idea would be fiercely propounded on the Continent that the calculation of longitude was possible from the positioning of the stars. Already much influenced at home that this lunar method could be feasible, he would be further encouraged by his French connections, particularly with Louise de Kerouaille, Duchess of Portsmouth; their son would be created Duke of Richmond. Thus in 1675 he authorised the design of a Royal Observatory by the 30-year-old astronomer and architect, Christopher Wren, who had just completed rebuilding the City of London after the Great Fire of 1666. Gradually expanded, the Royal Observatory Greenwich was destined to become universally renowned as both the home of Greenwich Mean Time and the Prime Meridian of the World.

A very modest building on the spur of the hill with a house for the Royal Astronomer would be completed in 1676; from there tens of thousands of observations would be made, 'reaching for the stars'. For having consulted his leading astronomer, the Derbyshire-born clergyman John Flamsteed, Charles II had discovered that there were no 'modern' reliable tables of the motions of the moon or charting of the fixed stars; as opposed to the revolving planets.

Already, just two years after his return, he had given his patronage to the Royal Society of London for Improving Natural Knowledge; initially a 'Group of Thinkers' who had been meeting informally since 1645, while the Civil War raged. Among the founder members of this very august and prestigious institution now with around 800 Fellows, were one Mr Christopher Wren and a Mr Robert Boyle, later to be the Earl of Orrery. He would write *The Skeptical Chymist*, among much else scientific, and provide the patronage and subsequently his name for the development of a 'clockwork' planet system; originally devised by the leading timepiece maker of his day, George Graham, of London.

Knowledge of the 'heavens above' was growing rapidly. Galileo had seen craters on the moon and found the Milky Way to be a collection of stars; Jupiter, the largest planet in the solar system some 470 million miles away (756 million Km), had four moons or satellites then identified – Io, Europa, Ganymede and Callisto. As we all know, Galileo also found that the Earth's nearest planet Venus, 163 million miles (262 million Km) away, had phases denoting possible orbiting of the sun 94 million miles away (152 million Km) on which he also saw 'spots'. These are now identified as areas of intense electromagnetism and possibly responsible for some of our bad weather.

Meanwhile, down below at Greenwich, because of economic considerations the new Royal Observatory was built on the foundations of Duke Humphrey's old watch-tower, later Greenwich Castle; unfortunately 13.5 degrees wide of the true north/south meridian. Many recycled materials from the Tower of London and Tilbury Docks were used, including decayed royal gunpowder and the stout poles of ships' spars, normally supporting sails, were detailed to support the state-of-the-art long telescopes. Finished within a year at a cost of approximately £520 9sh 1d, the total sum slightly exceeded the monarch's handout of £500.

Approximately 150 ft (46 m) above sea level, the Royal Observatory Greenwich became the workplace and centre for science for several centuries until the late 1920s onwards. By then some of the activities had been transferred elsewhere, due to interference from pollution. Magnetic readings suffered distortion as London expanded with railways and electric tram systems; a generating station was built by Greenwich Peninsula. The outbreak of World War II would provide further impetus for relocation. The scientific observations would eventually be re-established at Herstmonceux in Sussex, far removed from the air and light pollution of the capital. In 1960, the Royal Observatory we see today on 'Clock Hill' was affiliated to the National Maritime Museum situated in the park below. Then, accorded the prefix 'Old', the Royal Observatory buildings would house splendid exhibits of the early pioneering days of astronomy and more importantly, nights; the superbly crafted and functional scientific inventions encompassing many centuries and countries.

In 1990 the Royal Observatory moved from Herstmonceux to Cambridge but closed in 1998; the decision having been taken by its funding body, the Particle Physics and Astronomy Research Council (PPARC) to terminate its observational work; the function of the 'Public Understanding of Science' was transferred back to Greenwich. Most observing is now done at the Northern Hemisphere Observatory in the Canary Island of La Palma. In Sussex, the Herstmonceux Science Centre now incorporates the Laser Satellite Tracking Centre; able to pinpoint satellites to within a few feet (1 m) within its six domes. However, generally only three domes are open to the public.

The Old Royal Observatory proudly reverted to its original name of the Royal Observatory Greenwich. Much that was used there, when previously operational, has been returned. From a total of 7000 items, a selection of globes, astrolabes, orreries, sundials, sandglasses, clocks, chronometers and telescopes are on display for our indulgence, appreciation and wonderment. Specialist viewing of items is also available on application. The living area of John Flamsteed's home can also be explored. The stupendous achievements of John Harrison are recognised in an adjacent gallery, below which is the very informative Time Gallery. A subsidy from the PPARC allows provision of an Astronomical Information Unit and Search Station. A constantly updated Internet site, the Royal Observatory Astroweb, is situated in the interactive Arthur Weller Gallery of Modern Astronomy; located in the Meridian Building on the first floor and provided with technology generously donated by a former trustee of that name. The post of Astronomer Royal remains; appointed by the Sovereign on advice from the Prime Minister.

A new Astronomy Centre is envisaged in an upgraded South Building; built in 1899, beyond the Meridian Building, to support an additional telescope. State-of-the-art video technology is contemplated, focusing on the night skies, improved educational and visitor facilities and possible re-opening of the dome of the Planetarium presently housed within. It is reported that this would double the space at the ROG, allowing three new galleries for modern astronomy and more space in the older part for viewing of the historic collections. It is contemplated that a computer room would provide link-up to the National Schools Observatory network and contact with the Challenger Learning Centre at Leicester and John Moore's University in Liverpool.

Dr Robert Massey of the ROG represents London and the south-east for the National Schools Observatory (NSO) network. The study of astronomy is now encouraged in schools to promote interest in the study of science and engineering and as a basis for other subjects. The NSO has a series of workshops and fosters on-line learning. For over a decade John Moore's University, Liverpool, has been involved with the production of telescopes (Telescope Technologies Ltd); the Liverpool Telescope (LT) was shipped out to the Canaries in November 2001.

The NMM Trustee and former cosmologist and computer software specialist, Dr Martin 'Dill' Foulkes, has bought two further telescopes sited in Australia and Hawaii; these will be controlled 'live' via the internet.

The robotic telescopes do not need a large team of technical support and cost £2million. Their mirrors stand 8.5 metres tall with diameters of 2 metres.

Nearer home stargazing is far from over at the Royal Observatory Greenwich. In 1971, the great refracting telescope, then the largest in Britain with a diameter of 28 inches (70 cm) was returned from Herstmonceux. Crane-cuddled, it hovered in the sky before being lowered into the opened 'onion dome' of the Meridian Building. Officially superseded by the march of progress, the telescope functions still, giving pleasure to many at special events organised to explore the night sky. It is said that 'stunning images of moon and planets can be seen on clear nights'... despite it being over a hundred years old!

THE ROYAL OBSERVATORY GREENWICH
THE PRIME MERIDIAN OF THE WORLD
– 0.00 DEGREES LONGITUDE

(Latitude 51 Degrees 28 Minutes)

By the main entrance of the Royal Observatory, on the wall of the courtyard, is the very remarkable Shepherd Galvano-Magnetic Clock 24-hour dial, co-ordinating the solar and sidereal time as calculated by the stars; the term 'galvano' was then used for 'electric'. The hour hand marks 0 for midnight at the top of the dial and XII for noon at the base. This was first clock to show Greenwich Mean Time to the public in 1852, and still continues to do so. It was one of the 'slave' clocks linked to the new and innovative electric master clock supplied to the Royal Observatory in 1852 at a cost of £70 by Charles Shepherd of Leadenhall Street, London. Like the Time Ball, it is now controlled by the GMT Accurist Clock in the main entrance of the Meridian Building. On the wall beneath this remarkable clock is the now obsolete Public British Imperial Standards of Length in yards, feet and inches, mounted around 1866 for those wishing to verify measurements on tools.

But beyond the gate, and certainly not obsolete, is the Prime Meridian at longitude 0.00 degrees, pronouncing the division of the eastern and western hemispheres as defined by the Airy Transit Circle Telescope in the Meridian Building itself. It is simply denoted, infinitesimally proportional to the complex Herculean labours required for its achievement, by a metal strip a few inches below the surface of the courtyard with the names of sixty cities and their longitude east and west of Greenwich on either side.

On this is based the Mean Solar Time Unit, otherwise Greenwich Local Time or Greenwich Mean Time (GMT). There can be a discrepancy of up to 16 minutes when solar or sundial time is compared to clock time; due to the Earth's tilt of some 23.5 degrees on its axis to its plane of orbit and the varying speeds of the orbit itself around the sun. The average official measurements are 23 hours and 56 minutes for the daily rotation of the Earth and 365.25 days for the length of the Earth's orbit over one year around the sun.

You can have a certificate commemorating your visit, costing around £1.00. Admittedly, the occasion is neither as hot, nor perhaps as hilarious, as crossing the division of the northern and southern hemispheres can be when at sea, but a tour of John Flamsteed's home can compensate handsomely. It was the official home of the Royal Astronomers from 1676 to 1948. If you are in the courtyard at 12.55 hours, you will see the Time Ball aloft on Flamsteed House reach the top of its shaft below the weathervane at 12.58, then pause until exactly 13.00 hours and drop down to the base. Approximately 5 ft in diameter (1.5 m), it was made of leather when first installed in 1833 but replaced with aluminium in 1919 after being damaged by stormy weather. Tradition is still agreeably retained. It is said that when the signalling of Greenwich Mean Time began in 1833, as a daily routine to the ships below on the Thames, the Royal Observatory staff were too busy making their observations at midday to manually operate the Time Ball's machinery.

Below the Time Ball, we can glimpse through the tall windows of Flamsteed House the ladders placed to accommodate the long refracting telescopes which 'bent' the light; their lens 2.5 inches in diameter (6 cm). A plaque on the wall commemorates Charles II. To the right is the 'Camera Obscura', closeted in a minute turret; the darkened chamber allows us to see the images projected onto a viewing table. On the outside and facing the courtyard is the family tombstone of Edmund Halley, who served as the second Royal Astronomer from 1720 to 1742. This was restored by the Admiralty and transferred from St Margaret's Church at nearby Lee in 1854; a replica being provided for the original grave.

John Flamsteed and his wife, Margaret, are buried together in

Burstow Church in Sussex, where he also held the living as Rector; she was the granddaughter of his predecessor. Astronomers often took Holy Orders then. The village has not changed much. And neither has Flamsteed House, to any significant extent. Designed and described by Christopher Wren as "For the Observator's habitation…and a little for Pompe"; refurbished and officially opened by the Queen in 1960. The courtyard outside, however, one day in 1712 witnessed the frenzy and fury of the normally dour John Flamsteed, as he publicly burnt three hundred copies, three-quarters of his first observations, published without his consent. (Ref. Finale B)

THE ROYAL OBSERVATORY GREENWICH

FLAMSTEED HOUSE: HOME AND WORKPLACE TO THE FIRST ROYAL ASTRONOMER

"To apply himself with the utmost care and diligence to the rectifying of the tables of the motions of the heavens, and the places of the fixed stars, so as to find out the so much-desired longitude of places for the perfecting of the art of navigation..."

(Task entrusted to 28-year-old John Flamsteed by Charles II, 1675.)

If Mrs and Mrs Flamsteed were around today they would no doubt be interested, and perhaps amazed, to see so many people still coming to visit their modest home, now the oldest part of the Royal Observatory Greenwich. The magnificent views, from the north façade overlooking Greenwich Park, on a fine day can reach as far as the Tower of London upriver and the old Royal Docks at Woolwich downriver.

No doubt, too, that they would be intrigued to know that their lives and times are often re-enacted by professional actors; the Royal Observatory runs a very varied and instructive programme of events throughout the year, especially during school holidays. And they would probably be delighted to know that a computer can now instantaneously predict, to within an accuracy of a yard or metre, where the Prime Meridian is located by using the Differential Global Positioning System; and that a team from Greenwich University is busy searching out the English countryside and planting native species of trees along its length. Sometime in the not so distant future, it is envisaged, we will be able to grope our way 270 miles (434 Km) along the Prime Meridian from East Yorkshire via aspen, willow, oak and juniper to East Sussex.

John Flamsteed, in his day, assessed the true north/south meridian to be running through his back garden where he 'set up shop'. He had a salary of £100 annually, plus £26 for an assistant, from the Office of Ordnance. His work was considered a lowly occupation and he provided his own instruments; an expensive business for a relatively poor man. His 7 ft (2 m) mural sextant, with a graduated metal strip shaped in an arc of the sixth part of a circle, was equipped with two telescopic sights. His 7 ft (2 m) quadrant, shaped like a quarter of a circle, had a single telescopic sight. By measuring the angular distance between pairs of stars he recorded the position of the brightest stars. The first astronomer to measure systematically with telescopic sightings, he made his first 20,000 observations between 1676 and 1690.

By the time John Flamsteed died in 1719, he had made another 28,000 observations. A small legacy from his father enabled him to purchase a 10 ft (3 m) wall-mounted quadrant costing some £120; he then repeated many of his observations to obtain absolute accuracy. The mural arc with an angle of 140 degrees could, we are told, 'Cover all the stars from the Pole to the Horizon'.

He worked unceasingly, plagued by ill-health since childhood, in little more than a garden shed – The Quadrant – the shutters drawn back night-long. He was obliged to teach on the side, reluctantly, to eke out his meagre funds which were supplemented with a stipend from the parish of Burstow. Possibly this lifestyle with its attendant sleep deprivation had a bearing on the alleged rather unfortunate tendency to quarrel with some colleagues. He considered the study of astronomy essential 'to understand the mind of God', and was more than a little peeved not to have a personal pew allotted to him when St Alfege's church was rebuilt, after collapsing in a storm in 1710.

The panelled rooms in which the Flamsteeds lived, above a basement, are now painted cream; various windows are blocked due to the building of the adjacent exhibition galleries. Some of the old oak furniture might perhaps be familiar to Elizabeth I, but not the pendulum clocks ticking quietly away in corners, one a hooded wall clock by Thomas Tompion. From their living quarters, you will be guided up a narrow staircase to the splendid Great Star Room, the purpose-built Wren's 'little pompe'; otherwise known as the Octagon. This, however, could only be used for general viewing; it was built on the foundations of the old watchtower and was not on the true north-south axis. Also, there was no overhead opening, so it was not suitable for positional astronomy.

On discovering this, the lamenting John Flamsteed retreated to the back garden; starting his observations from there he would go on to form an accurate basis for a catalogue of northern stars. Meanwhile, colleague Edmund Halley, then a friend and much in his company, sailed south to St Helena with the blessing of Charles II where he commenced charting the stars in the southern hemisphere. On return to England in 1678, Edmund Halley became friendly with Isaac Newton, generously publishing his *Principia*. He further applied Newton's Laws of Motion to his calculations of the orbits of comets and noted the periodicity of some, particularly one in 1682. Halley's Comet still recurs every 76 years, as he so accurately predicted.

The Octagon Room, also known as the 'Camera Stellata', became a fashionable salon of 'hands-on astronomy', especially useful for observing eclipses and comets. Soon after John Flamsteed moved in, it also became home for a pair of clocks that ticked uniquely every two seconds and needed winding only once a year. They were the brainchild of Thomas Tompion; baptised in 1639 at Northill in Bedfordshire and possibly first working as a blacksmith. In 1676 he was appointed clockmaker to the Royal Observatory Greenwich. He would go on to become the 'father of English clock-making' and Master of the Clockmakers Company. He was also known for very significant contributions to the progress in watch construction; particularly that of the cylinder escapement with horizontal wheel, making possible the advent of 'flat' watches.

His designs for the Octagon Room's timepieces were unique in that each had a 13 ft pendulum (4 m) concealed behind the floor-to-ceiling walnut panelling. It was correctly considered that a smaller swing would ensure a more precise measurement of time. He also devised the 'dead beat' escapement which stopped the wheels in the gearing recoiling backwards with each swing of the pendulum. His design would be adapted for domestic use as our familiar long-case grandfather clock; there is one circa 1737 in the Octagon Room today.

Thomas Tompion's two revolutionary timekeepers enabled John Flamsteed to quickly prove that the Earth did rotate at an even rate, a calculation superseded only in the 1930s with the discovery of quartz-crystal mechanisms for perfecting frequency control.

Replica clocks are there now, behind the mellowed walls hung with life-size portraits of brothers Charles II and James II. The original workings of one clock are in an adjacent showcase; the other found its way to the British Museum. For when the widowed Mrs Flamsteed sold up in 1719, she stripped the house bare, making sure that absolutely nothing was left for her husband's successor; the by then loathed Edmund Halley who had secretly connived with Isaac Newton and edited her husband's incomplete observations for 'pirate' publication.

For John Flamsteed, academic rigour had been the absolute priority. Pressure from the scientific establishment to peruse the results of his incomplete observations meant nothing to him. Isaac Newton was insistent that he publish; he and his contemporaries at the Royal Society had research of their own to complete about the development of the universe. John Flamsteed's data was essential for this. The support of Queen Anne was enlisted and in 1712 the *Historia Coelestis Britannica* was published, but with many errors and abridgements; the printer's bill being picked up by Prince George of Denmark just before he died in 1708. However, with the accession of George I in 1714, who first set foot in England at Greenwich, John Flamsteed had more influence at Court. Managing to get hold of 300 of the 400 copies, he delivered them to the flames outside Flamsteed House 'as a sacrifice to heavenly truth…'

With the proceeds of the sale of her husband's belongings, Margaret Flamsteed triumphantly published the monumental *Historia Coelestis*

Britannica in 1725; finally corrected and completed six years after his death by her husband's two assistants. There is a copy of a 1st Edition just inside Flamsteed House today. The initial two volumes included the whole of his 30,000 approved observations and the third, the *British Catalogue* of nearly 3,000 stars, would form the basis of modern star catalogues. Subsequent Royal Astronomers would use this material, over the next four decades, as the basis of the first *Nautical Almanac* which would eventually commence annual publication in 1767. From then on, navigators had access to the exact angles between the moon and certain fixed stars, at any time throughout the year. The moon tables were based on the work of the German astronomer Johann Tobias Mayer (1723-62) who submitted to the British Government a few years before he died lunar tables which Astronomer Royal James Bradley found to be sufficiently accurate, it is recorded, to determine the Moon's phase to 75" and consequently longitude at sea to half a degree. A London edition was published in 1770 and a revision edited by Astronomer Royal Nevil Naskelyne in 1787.

After considerable calculations, the time at Greenwich could be deduced. Greenwich Mean Time had been charted in the skies above, but down below on the oceans a sea-going clock that kept accurate time when set to it had yet to surface.

THE ROYAL OBSERVATORY GREENWICH

FLAMSTEED HOUSE: GALLERIES OF TIME AND JOHN HARRISON'S VERY NOTABLE WATCH

"But they still say a watch can be but a watch…and that the performance of mine (though nearly to truth itself) must be altogether a deception"

(Lament of John Harrison, 1763.)

The 'race against time' to accurately tell the time at sea during the late 17th and early 18th centuries was elusive, extensive and expensive; it took six decades and culminated with 'man and machine versus the moon'. More than a little acrimoniously, man and machine emerged the victor, pioneered by the practical, tenacious and profoundly industrious clockmaker, John Harrison from Lincolnshire; he would infallibly demonstrate that longitude could be calculated to within half a degree during a trial sea voyage to the West Indies in 1764.

Having initially experimented with the new 'pendulum technology', he developed a uniquely fast-ticking, precision watch which would be adapted and commercially developed as the science of marine chronometry. It has been said that John Harrison's contribution to the solution of the 'longitude problem' ranks with the importance of the magnetic compass in the 13th century and the development of radar in the 20th.

Leading off from the Octagon Room in Flamsteed House today, you will find a gallery dedicated to John Harrison; included among the exhibits his last journal, recording, in a neat sloping hand, some very eventful meetings. But pride of place belongs to a large silver 'pocket watch' of 5-inch diameter (12.5 cm) with a very clear white dial. The now famous, but at first infamous H4, to be copied as K1 and travel the world with Captain Cook as the first-ever marine chronometer. It is not shown working as this would require periodic withdrawal for servicing.

Alongside are John Harrison's meticulously crafted and magnificently executed three large brass clocks; the masterpieces H1, H2 and H3, still vigorously working. We have the advantage of a computer model to explain their sophistications. Nearby is a portrait of him holding a small pocket watch which he designed and commissioned from his watchmaker friend, John Jeffrys. The original is also on display alongside, together with some of his other designs and drawings. Made only for his personal use, this watch, known as the Jeffrys Watch, provided the catalyst for John Harrison's final triumph of H4; designed with a relatively large, high-frequency, heavy balance wheel capable of independence of the motion of a ship, plus a sophisticated temperature compensation. The resulting combination was a timepiece with an accommodation of only 5-10 seconds a day. Uniquely made of brass and steel and weighing only 3 pounds (1.5 Kg), the breakthrough H4 would eventually be described as 'the forerunner of all precision watches and probably the most important timekeeper ever made'.

John Harrison first visited London in 1730 with his pioneering designs of a bimetallic 'grid-iron' pendulum, ingenuously incorporating the combined wires to compensate for temperature expansion. He went immediately to the Royal Observatory to see Royal Astronomer Edmund Halley who had by then been holder of the post for eleven years – an auspicious occasion for the homespun, self-educated John Harrison, born at Foulby in Yorkshire in 1693; son of a carpenter, later estate surveyor. Edmund Halley listened, was impressed and sent him down to George Graham in the City; eventually he, too, became very interested in his visitor's ideas. They talked long and dined. John Harrison was made a substantial loan to continue his work.

On moving to London a few years later, John Harrison first lived at Leather Lane, leaving behind his cottage on the Barton Road at

Barrow upon Humber in North Lincolnshire where his father, Henry, had been a much respected parish clerk for several decades and he had done so much of his brilliant and pioneering experimental work; the dwelling would be regrettably destroyed only in 1970, while awaiting a preservation order. John Harrison's ideas would be over a century ahead of the times and provoke the incredulity – and derisions – of many. The story of the search for longitude by means of a sea-going clock and other methods, some farcical, is well displayed and documented in the gallery devoted to him. Excellent books have been written as well as a riveting, award-winning TV drama series entitled simply 'Longitude'. (Ref. Part II. John Harrison – Trials of Clocking Time at Sea.)

Nearby John Harrison's clocks you will see a small exhibition dedicated to the contribution of the eminent amateur horologist, Lieutenant Rupert T Gould, in restoring the masterpieces to their former glory. Why they had remained undiscovered, gathering dirt in the cellars of the Royal Observatory until the 1920s, having been ignominiously transferred there by a horse and unsprung cart from John Harrison's house in Red Lion Square near Holborn in 1766, is an astonishing story. Even more astounding is the fact that John Harrison was never allowed access to them again. Rupert Gould's expert researches were published in 1923 as the definitive and still-unrivalled *Marine Chronometer*. John Harrison's achievements were developed in England by the noted clockmakers and rivals, John Arnold, an expert in precision timing, and Thomas Earnshaw, known also for his work on the cylindrical balance spring and detached *detente* escapement.

Using funds awarded by the Board of Longitude, eventually wound up in 1828, over 1000 'box' chronometers would be commercially produced; three being eventually apportioned per ship. Their simplified technology and state-of-the-art manufacturing guaranteed models a tenth of the original price, without minimising the performance or quality.

In the Chronometer showcase in the Harrison Gallery you can see the original workings of the K1 and K2 models; made for the Admiralty by Marcum Kendall of London, hence the K. The first copy of H4, the K1 model taken on trial by Captain Cook on his second voyage, cost £500 – equivalent to £25,000 or more today. The later model K3 cost £100 and was taken by Cook on his third and final voyage; it was also used by George Vancouver when navigating the north-west coast of America. Subsequently, the Royal Observatory Greenwich would become the testing centre of new models; a year of rigorous trials being required and including subjection to high temperatures for long periods.

The Royal Navy survey vessel *HMS Beagle*, when voyaging with Charles Darwin aboard from 1832-35, had no less than twenty-two chronometers strategically placed throughout; plus a brief to systematically chart the South American coast, after the correct longitude for Rio had been established. The Beagle undertook the first ever voyage given sailing orders by the Admiralty that wind observations should be taken using the Beaufort Wind Scale. A brass 'patent log' belonging to the Surveyor of that vessel, John Stokes, can be seen in the Navigation Gallery in the National Maritime Museum near the K1 and sextant of the style used by Captain Cook. It was invented for the automatic measurement of knots and resembles a miniature torpedo, 12-18 inches in length (30–40 cm) with 'tail fins'; three small numbered dials each approximately 1 inch in diameter (2.5 cms) are placed on one side. John Harrison would eventually receive his long-awaited financial recognition from the Board of Longitude, but only after intervention by the Monarch and Parliament. He died a few years later, in 1776, on his 83rd birthday at Red Lion Square and was buried in Hampstead Church.

He would probably be pleased to know that in the Time Gallery, on the floor beneath his displays, you can hear the mellow and almost hypnotic ticking of an 1888 Gillet Turret Clock; a three-legged 'gravity escapement' regulates the release of the energy source. The same system similarly controls the famous clock, fronting the 13.5-ton bell of Big Ben in St Stephen's Tower, Westminster. For John Harrison had been an expert bell-ringer at his parish church of Holy Trinity at Barrow on Humber where he was also choir master and viol player. Finding time to note, however, the large swing of the bells through an arc of 250 degrees, he had used this calculation as a basis for his pendulum experiments. He had also intuitively realised that the high frequency of musical instruments could influence timepiece design. However, as he and others came painfully to realise, pendulum timepieces could never cope on the moving oceans for they relied on gravity to provide steady control of the clock's wheels. Also in the Time Gallery, you may notice an electric clock. They appeared around 1840, the pendulums having electromagnetic coils in the bob. Two decades earlier the Danish Hans Christian Oersted had noted that a compass needle is deflected when brought near a wire carrying an electric current; in fact, electromagnetism.

A year before Queen Victoria came to the throne in 1837, the Royal Observatory relayed Greenwich Mean Time to all principal chronometer makers in London; a service carried out in person by John Belville. His daughter, Ruth, inherited the task. Referred to as the 'Greenwich Time Lady', she verified GMT from the Shepherd Gate Clock and travelled into London every Monday morning with it by the simple expedient of a large pocket chronometer in her handbag; affectionately named 'Arnold' in honour of its designer, John Arnold.

From 1852 onwards, Greenwich Mean Time was distributed throughout the country by electric telegraph, particularly necessary for the strict timetables of the new national railway system as 'local time' caused much confusion; passengers of today have yet to hear that explanation.

The one o'clock signal from Greenwich led to a nationwide system of time balls, cannons, bells and needles. By the turn of the century, miniature electrically-operated time balls had pride of place in many business offices in the City of London. By then the pioneering Italian-Irish and future Nobel Prize winner Gugliremo Marconi had been experimenting with 'wireless' waves on Salisbury Plain and across the Bristol Channel. No doubt he would be gratified to know that some 60 years later the great concave-shaped discs of the radio-telescope, designed specifically for collecting and focusing radio waves for the University of Manchester, began to grace the skyline at Jodrell Bank, in Cheshire.

However, inside the Royal Observatory, the 'writing on the wall' in the Time Gallery will inform us that in 1906 came the first public broadcast and, in 1924, the six famous 'pips' which still precede every major BBC bulletin. They were instigated by Royal Astronomer Frank Dyson and the electric-clock pioneer, Frank Home Jones. The previous year, the chimes of Big Ben at Westminster had been broadcast for the first time; a sound already familiar to Londoners since 1859 when the clock was designed by the multi-talented Edmund Denison, later Lord Grimthorpe. The bell behind the famous façade was reputedly named after the rotund Commissioner of Works for the House of Commons, Sir Benjamin Hall.

The 'speaking-clock' service began in 1936; the signals were sent by landline to the BBC, then at Savoy Hill by the Strand. The two clocks used are exhibited: No 2012 (sidereal) was originally made for a transit of Venus in 1874 and used until 1949 when the more sophisticated quartz was implemented; No 2016 (GMT) was for back-up. The lucky owners of 'wirelesses' were able to count down the seconds to the hour and revel in the luxury of setting their clocks and watches accurately at home. William Shortt's Master Clock No 6, with its 'free' pendulum swinging in a partial vacuum, controlled Britain's radio time signals from the Royal Observatory for the period 1927-43. The pendulum clock would reach a very high degree of precision during the first quarter of the 20th century; the rates of the best were accurate to 0.001 seconds per day. Also on show is the Precision Pendulum Clock circa 1969; used until the 1970s by the Moscow Research Station for reasons of economy, it was much less expensive than quartz which by then was being used in wristwatches.

The BBC now uses two atomic clocks. We are now four million 'pips' on with an extra one thrown in occasionally as a 'leap' every two to three years; the rotation of the Earth varies and atomic caesium must always be kept in check by Greenwich Mean Time. The vibrations of a caesium atom are nine billion per second and the International Standard for the length of a second is based on this. An atomic oscillator combined with a clock can emit a rate constant to 1 microsecond (1 millionth) per day.

There is a model of the Caesium Atomic Clock circa 1973 exhibited in the Time Gallery. While no doubt the silicon chip within manipulated electric signals with split second accuracy, this modern 'marvel' resembles only a squat computer desktop unit with a small dial and control panel. But now on show near the door into the garden is the still-under-development and much more exciting to view Caesium Fountain Atomic Clock; the bright red and blue 'atoms' excitedly chase each other round the visible interior – aiming to 'correct' time even better than one second per million years.

THE ROYAL OBSERVATORY GREENWICH
THE HOME OF TIME ROSE GARDEN

I saw Eternity the other night,
Like a great ring of pure and endless light,
All calm, as it was bright;
And round beneath it, Time in hours, days, years
Driv'n by the spheres
Like a vast shadow moved; in which all the world
And all her train were hurl'd.

From *The World* by Henry Vaughan, 1622-1695. (Poet, Mystic and Medical Practitioner; twin brother of Thomas Vaughan, Poet, Mystic and Chemist.)

In the small quadrangle of garden with an old apple tree, between Flamsteed House and the Meridian Building, lies the Home of Time Rose Garden; particularly delightful in summer and so petite that it could grace the rear of many a suburban residence. But there the comparison ends. For it was here, on 1 October 1998, that representatives of the twenty-five nations that had originally voted to adopt Greenwich Mean Time at the International Meridian Conference held in 1884 in Washington, USA, met to honour the event over a century later and dedicate the official planting of the Home of Time Rose Garden.

In 1884 the delegates at the Washington conference had decided on a single world meridian, based at Greenwich 0.00 degrees, and that all longitude would be calculated both east and west of that meridian up to 180 degrees. Thus, the Greenwich calculation of 0.00 degrees became the Prime Meridian of world time and subsequent time zones. For centuries the fixing of the east-west meridian had been the prerogative of the mapmaker or cartographer. Claudius Ptolemy in AD 150 had decided on the Canary Islands, probably at Ferro, and his decision persisted for over 1500 years. Situated 67 miles (108 Km) off north-west Africa, this area was the furthest point of western civilization; Columbus knew the islands well. Among the many other places considered and used at times over the centuries were Cape Verde, Toledo in Spain and islands in the mid-Atlantic favoured by the Flemish geographer and cartographer, Gerardus Mercator, who used a picture of the Greek god Atlas holding up the pillars separating Earth from heaven as his frontispiece when publishing books of charts.

The Washington Conference in 1884 was not the first international meeting to consider a world meridian, but it was the last. The delegates also agreed their respective countries would adopt a Universal Day which would also be a 'Mean Solar Day', beginning at the moment of Mean Midnight at Greenwich and calculated on a 24-hour clock. Every twelve hours, one calendar day would be added when travelling westwards, and likewise subtracted when travelling eastwards. Nautical and astronomical days would begin at Mean Midnight; the Decimal System would be encouraged for calculating the divisions of time and space.

The nations opting for Greenwich Mean Time in 1884 were Austria, Hungary, Chile, Colombia, Costa Rica, Denmark, Germany, Great Britain, Guatemala, Hawaii, Italy, Japan, Liberia, Mexico, The Netherlands, Paraguay, Russia, San Domingo, Salvador, Spain, Sweden and Norway, Switzerland, Turkey, the USA and Venezuela. One country, San Domingo, voted against. Brazil and France abstained. It was also agreed that the world would be officially divided into 24 one-hour zones; each responding to 15 degrees longitude with the cumulative distance up to 180 degrees, or twelve hours in time, east and west of Greenwich. This has remained; some slight adjustments during the succeeding century have been made by continents with large land masses for convenience. Some countries have compromised with half-hourly differences. Western Europe would adopt a time-zone system one hour faster than GMT and East Europe two hours faster. Seasonal variations have also been adopted on occasions, such as British Summertime.

By 1884, the USA had already adopted GMT for their large nationwide time-zone system. Previously, in 1870, the American Professor Charles F Dowd had by then proposed that the Greenwich Meridian should be used as the basis of what became the world time-zone system; a decision backed by Canada which, like the USA, had vast areas and wide differences in longitude. British Standard Time was easily instigated in the UK as the total difference in longitude measurements equated to only thirty minutes of time; GMT became official by Royal Assent in 1880, only four years before the Washington conference. And a mere twelve years before Professor Dowd's proposal in 1870, the largest ship then built had to be expediently launched sideways in 1858 at Burrell's Wharf, Millwall; just across the Thames from the Royal Observatory.

She was Isambard Kingdom Brunel's third and largest ship, the *Great Eastern*, with a length of 680 ft (207 m); well able to accommodate the thousands of tons of underwater cable required to reach across the Atlantic Ocean to the USA from Britain and able to sustain an electric current capable of transmission of telegraphy by Morse Code and of course, Greenwich Mean Time. It is on record that the Greenwich time signal was received twice a day on the *Great Eastern*, thus making the accurate calculation of longitude possible. Isambard Brunel died ten days before her maiden voyage and never knew of the subsequent success of his great ship, sometimes referred to as *Leviathan*. There are paintings of the remarkable 32,000-ton *Great Eastern* in the London Maritime and the All Hands Galleries in the National Maritime Museum. Although she was eventually broken up, the production of submarine cabling from Greenwich continued for well over a century, until 1979. The final electric cable used by the *Great Eastern* was insulated with the flexible thickened gum of 'gutta percha' obtained from the latex of the *Sapotaceae* and *Palaquium* varieties of tree in the southern hemispheres, and encased with the more mundane brass plating. The 'gutta percha' motif may still be visible on nearby buildings at the Lovell and Enderby's wharves beyond Ballast Quay where the cable-laying ships were moored off Greenwich Peninsula.

Several other transatlantic attempts had been fruitless. One previous cable, although completely laid, had burned out almost immediately due to too large a current being transmitted in ignorance; the celebration party was still in progress in America at the time. The eventual link-up came as a great relief during 1865-66 when GMT could be cabled to America

Also a vital consideration at the Washington conference when officially establishing the Prime Meridian at Greenwich as the universal choice, was the fact that over 70% of the world's commerce depended on sea-charts which used Greenwich 0.00 degrees longitude as the prime meridian. Apart from the publication of the *Nautical Almanac*, the advent of the chronometer and the epic explorations of Captain James Cook, the survey vessels of the Royal Navy, such as Darwin's *Beagle*, had for decades journeyed rigorously and dangerously to all parts of the globe. Assiduously they charted coastlines, known and unknown, often sailing in the small brigs unflatteringly referred to as 'coffin ships', but their results were published using the Greenwich Meridian, available to all.

However, other countries had also been busy on the seas and in the sky. Two centuries before the Washington Conference, the Paris Observatory, when inaugurated in 1671, astutely appointed Professor Giovanni Demenico Cassini of the University of Bologna as Director. He would be the first of four generations of his family to officially hold the post and developed Galileo's observations of Jupiter's moons and eclipses hoping to use them for the determination of longitude at sea. His first tables showed the position of the four moons, providing a precise celestial timekeeper at 19.00 every evening. He was also a keen observer of Saturn; in 1997 a space probe bearing his name took off on a four-year journey to that planet.

The French delegate chose to abstain at the Washington conference; his country also wished Great Britain to adopt the metric system. In

1891 Paris Mean Time was adopted by French law. France would be the first country to broadcast the time in 1910. The world now uses 'Co-ordinated Universal Time', referred to as UTC, determined by 200 atomic clocks in thirty countries. This is the time officially given out on radio signals. The clocks are controlled by the International Bureau of Weights and Measures in Paris and the time distributed via the Bureau International de l'Heure. The present sophistication of the calculations is such that various other corrections to longitude due to polar motion, lunar effect and seasonal variation, once impossible to ascertain, can now also be computed and distributed to observatories.

But however advanced the degree of sophistication, the UTC is based on Greenwich Mean Time.

THE ROYAL OBSERVATORY GREENWICH
MERIDIAN BUILDING AND PLANETARIUM – TELESCOPES IN TRANSIT

"To begin for all the world at the moment of mean midnight of the original meridian..."

(*The Universal Day*, as defined at the Washington Conference, 1884.)

THE ROYAL ASTRONOMERS

John Flamsteed	1675-1719
Edmond Halley	1720-1742
James Bradley	1742-1762
Nathaniel Bliss	1762-1764
Nevil Maskelyne	1765-1811
John Pond	1811-1835
Sir George Biddell Airy	1835-1881
Sir William Christie	1881-1910
Sir Frank Dyson	1910-1933
Sir Harold Spencer Jones	1933-1955
Sir Richard Woolley	1956-1971
Sir Martin Ryle	1972-1982
Sir Francis Graham-Smith	1982-1990
Arnold Wolfendale	1991-1994
Sir Martin Rees	1995-

Entering via the side door from the Home of Time Rose Garden, you will see just inside a thin red line marking the west side of the former brick and timber shed, used by John Flamsteed for his original Greenwich Meridian. Known as the Quadrant, some of the original bricks are preserved nearby in the wall not far from a Degree Clock designed by him and made by Thomas Tompion. Several incumbents of the office of Royal Astronomer instigated other 'Greenwich

Meridians' as calculated by their own state-of-the-art telescopes. When Edmund Halley calculated his own meridian a few feet to the right of John Flamsteed's, the Quadrant was used as a pigeon loft for a while.

It is possible to view the rear garden where John Flamsteed positioned his 100 ft (30 m) well-telescope in 1676. Opposite on the outside back wall of the Meridian Building is the position of the Bradley Meridian as defined by the third Royal Astronomer, Gloucestershire-born James Bradley, using his 8 ft (2.5 m) transit telescope. James Bradley's meridian continued in official use as the Greenwich Meridian for the century 1750 to 1850. It would serve as the basis for the Anglo-French joint project to measure the distance between the Observatories in Paris and Greenwich in 1783 and also for the Ordnance Survey mapping begun in 1791; the first OS Map of the County of Kent being published a decade later. The Bradley Meridian is still used; to alter would mean re-surveying the entire British Isles, unless modern technology simplifies update.

The official Ordnance Survey Bench Mark G 1692, marking the Royal Observatory since 1921 as 152 ft (46 m) above the mean sea level at Newlyn in Cornwall, can be seen by the Shepherd Clock. The theodolite instrument used on the very first survey is displayed in the Bradley Meridian Room; made by Jesse Ramsden in 1791 who also invented the 'dividing engine' for assessing equal degree measurements of an arc. During the 18th and 19th centuries the very best of craftsman in London and elsewhere were becoming increasingly even more sophisticated in the execution of their products, as the exhibition cases splendidly portray in the Meridian Building.

The various Royal Astronomers and their limited but very able staffs also did much else. James Bradley encouraged the Board of Ordnance to build most of the present Meridian Building; the Royal Navy would also contribute substantially for the provision of new instruments. He would go on to discover the 'wobble' of the Earth on its axis every 19 years and the 'aberration of light' as the Earth moves around the sun; the theory of which was apparently triggered when sailing on the Thames and observing the shifting of the vane on the mast as the boat altered course. The controversial Nevil Maskelyne, who caused much annoyance to pioneer sea-going clockmaker John Harrison with his insistence that the astronomical lunar method was the only answer to the longitude problem, published the first *British Nautical Almanac and Astronomical Ephemeris for the Meridian of the Royal Observatory Greenwich'* a year after taking up the post in 1766.

France had produced a nautical almanac almost a century previously and some other countries would follow suit. Nevil Maskelyne had also published, in 1763, the *British Mariner's Guide*; a lifelong devotee of the practical application of astronomy to safe navigation, his other work and observations provided the basis for the density of the Earth being then calculated as 4.5 times that of water. The British *Nautical Almanac* became widely respected by mariners worldwide, including the Russian Navy. Based on Greenwich Mean Time, like so many seafarers charts then, it would be revised and adapted down the years.

He was succeeded by John Pond who not only increased the support staff from one to six assistants but also desired "hard workers and above all obedient drudges". He soon recognised that the age of the Greenwich quadrant had become a handicap and updated the equipment to include 'astronomical circles', which he had utilised himself previously for observations elsewhere. Pond also readily agreed to the suggestion that the help given to sailors by an experimental time ball, erected in Portsmouth Harbour entrance, should be implemented at Greenwich. Two years before retirement he published, in 1833, an acclaimed catalogue containing observations of over a thousand stars.

In 1835 the dynamic Sir George Biddell Airy, Professor of Mathematics and Astronomy at Cambridge, where he was Director of the University Observatory, arrived on the scene. By then the Greenwich Meridian had already extended eastwards albeit in a somewhat piecemeal fashion; the observational work then could never be sacrificed to closure for refurbishment. He would move the Greenwich Meridian to its fourth and final position approximately 19ft (6m) from the original John Flamsteed's Quadrant; an accommodation of only 1/50th of a second and a time too small for 19th century astronomers to measure. Today, exploring the very modestly-sized Halley's and Bradley's Meridian Rooms complete with some of George Graham's scientific clocks, the Astronomical Regulators for use with the 'transit telescopes' that were designed to 'sweep across the sky', you are soon confronted by the Airy Transit Circle Telescope. Installed in 1850 by Sir George Biddell Airy, it was soon recognised as the supremo. Two years previously he had purchased an 8-inch lens (20 cm) and proceeded to design a telescope around it. The result would be what we see today, still in its massive and almost 'Heath-Robinson' original mounting, able to swing through 360 degrees and weighing 2000 pounds (907 Kg).

Beneath the brickwork base the stargazer sat in a whitewashed trench-like slit just below ground level. Such was the sophistication of this Victorian engineering marvel more than aptly described as being ' like a large field gun', that not only could he swivel the telescope to which part of the north or south sky he was required to observe, but to determine a degree of accuracy to 1/100 of a second of an arc or 1/360 thousandths of degree; this was possible from a sequence of micrometer microscopes set on the axis. From where he sat a brass strip, denoting the Greenwich Meridian, extended out into courtyard. The first observation was made on 4 January 1851, three days later than intended due to bad weather; the same year as the Great Exhibition in Hyde Park. With its installation, the position of the Greenwich Meridian finally 'took root'; in fact where we see it today.

It was perhaps fortuitous that the establishment of the electric telegraph system in 1836 should be only a year after the appointment of Sir George Biddell Airy, so full of human dynamism himself. He first automated the Time Ball by using an electric signal. When it was blown down in a winter gale during 1855 his son, Hubert, painted a small watercolour of the event; this is now exhibited by the door to the Octagon Room in Flamsteed House.

In 1836, a personal courier service of issuing Greenwich Mean Time to the chronometer workshops of London was begun; simply by one of his twenty assistants, John Belville, carrying a large watch. GMT would eventually be extended to the Post Office and railways by 1847; essential for the Great Exhibition at Hyde Park where some six million people visited, a large majority travelling by train. In 1852 he synchronised all the clocks in the Royal Observatory from Charles Shepherd's new electric master clock and then transmitted GMT via the newly developing telegraph systems throughout Britain, and on request to any foreign observatories that applied for it. Sir George Biddell Airy was firmly convinced that GMT should be available to all; mooting the idea with practical steps that crossed the boundary of GMT's role, which began as an astronomical and navigational aid, to that of universal communication. No doubt he would be gratified today to know that Hawaii, home to the Foulkes telescope due to be linked up to the Royal Observatory Greenwich, is recorded on our home computers as GMT – 10.00 hours.

In 1851 a submarine cable was laid beneath the English Channel to France. In 1860 GMT reached India by a cable between Malta and Alexandria. As well as the *Great Eastern's* transatlantic submarine link-up in 1866 to the USA, Ireland was also similarly connected to Newfoundland. From 1870 time balls and public clocks at home and abroad received the GMT time from a signal operating through the nationalized Post Office telegraph system.

Sir George Biddell Airy, we are told, was a great believer in automation; and not only with astronomical instruments. He reputedly controlled his workforce as a factory manager, working them twelve hours a day and allegedly never keen to promote or pay well; partly because he felt there was little future for the majority. However, many staff at the Royal Observatory were also very talented.

One, Thomas Taylor, designed an alarm clock especially for astronomers. Several copies were made by William Johnson of London. You can see one, dated 1827, presently exhibited in the Hidden Treasures Gallery in the National Maritime Museum; there are quite distinct holes in the clock dial in which pins were inserted. The on-duty astronomer would be woken a few minutes before specified stars crossed the field of his telescope, allowing him to have a nap between vigils. Obviously not inclined to take naps himself between ideas, the redoubtable Sir George Biddell Airy went on to design a chronograph, or stop watch, for use specifically with his very own Airy Transit Circle Telescope that still defines longitude on its cross-hairs for public demonstrations.

In its heyday, it would make 600,000 official observations; the operator correcting the master clock to send out the time signal every hour by the most accurate system of time-measurement then known, that of the stars. It was eventually taken out of official service, after a century of use, in 1954. Exactly a century before, the Northumberland-born Sir George had established himself at a deep mine shaft in the neighbouring county of Durham, at South Shields, and by means of pendulum experiments at the top and bottom deduced the mean density of the Earth and updated it to be that of 6.5 times that of water.

He resigned in 1881, at the age of eighty, and spent the last eleven years of his life concentrating on lunar theory. Apart from his achievements at the Royal Observatory he had also discovered inequality in the motions of Venus and the Earth, attempted to correct his own astigmatism by a suitable cylindrical lens, formulated mathematical physics relating to the theory of light including that of rays in rainbows and had the central spot that contains most of the light flux in a microscope named after him as the Airy Disk. Not content with that, in 1857 he installed the bigger Equatorial Refracting Telescope with a lens of 12.8 inch (32.5 cm) made by Merz of Munich; to accommodate this, he extended the Meridian site eastwards by adding the octagonal Great Equatorial Building, easily visible by the present onion-shaped Telescope Dome. The main entrance to the Royal Observatory is now beneath.

Over a century later, the study of the stars progressed to the placing of telescopes not only on the high mountains of the world above the clouds, but also above the atmosphere as satellites and in space stations. Latterly, in 1987, the William Herschel telescope, 14 ft diameter (4 m) was installed at La Palma in the Canary Islands. Recently a team of four astronomers have been appointed to promote the new 'live' Royal Observatory Greenwich and 'bring modern astronomy' to the public. Climbing up to the Arthur Weller Gallery of Modern Astronomy and the Astroweb in the Meridian Building will show you how.

If you want to go further and see the Great Equatorial Refracting Telescope at close quarters, so-named because of its type of mounting and housed beneath the specially designed onion dome that replaced the Airy drum dome, then there is a spiral staircase of sixteen iron steps plus a little cautious walking around the parapet with grand views across London for diversion. This telescope weighing 1.5 tons was commissioned in the 1880s by Royal Astronomer William Christie from the Optical and Mechanical Works at Rathmines in Ireland. There, Mr Howard Grubb had just built the world's then largest refractor for the Royal Vienna Observatory. The Chance Bros of Birmingham were given the specialised job of casting the 28-inch diameter (70 cm) lenses; one of the only two manufacturers then able to supply such a highly sophisticated product.

This would still prove to be an arduous process; after sixteen individual casting failures and only after more than three years of effort were two discs of comparable quality produced. Mr Grubb (later Sir Howard) then indulged in nearly three years of relentless grinding and polishing until perfection was declared. Then, it is reported, the glass discs finally weighing 200 pounds (91 Kg) were sewn into felt-stuffed cushions and sealed in a box. This was placed in a second box lined with springs and freighted via a British and Irish Steam Packet bound for Holyhead. The next stage was a train to Euston and then a special 'sprung van' for the final lap to Greenwich; John Harrison had not been so privileged when Royal Astronomer Nevil Maskelyne transferred his precious clocks somewhat unceremoniously from his home in Red Lion Square to the Royal Observatory at the command of the Admiralty, their ownership by then in dispute.

After a long process of installation, the telescope was ready for used in June 1893 – more than eight years after commissioning. And it's still there for us to marvel and enjoy today; impregnable on the huge mounting originally belonging to the previous telescope of 1859, made by Ransomes and Sims of Ipswich. Now, it is used throughout the winter months for public and educational demonstrations and sessions with the amateur Friends' Flamsteed Astronomy Society.

The marvellous intricacies of its construction are highlighted today by video information; you may also be fortunate enough to be accompanied by one of the very knowledgeable volunteer guides. Excellent books and souvenirs are available in the Star Shop below; descent is via 39 steps on an iron spiral staircase or you can go back the way you came via the Arthur Weller Gallery. Beyond the Meridian Building the distinctive 'Halley's Comet' wind-vane aloft denotes the small Altazimuth Pavilion; known by the Arabic name meaning an 'instrument for determining altitude and heavenly bodies'. Erudite Arabian scholars, great cataloguers themselves, had so esteemed Ptolemy's works that by the 9th century his works became known collectively then, and still remain, as the 'Almagest', or *Al Megister*.

To the rear, comparatively massive and dominating the horizon, however, is the terracotta South Building designed as the New Physical Laboratory in 1899. It was opened as the Planetarium in 1965. A bust of John Flamsteed, resplendent on a frieze, oversees the entrance; the names of other famous astronomers and instrument makers are likewise honoured encircling the building. Just below the South

Building in the garden are the truncated remains of William Herschel's 40 ft (12 m) unique reflecting telescope, reposing under a translucent dome. He had moved to Slough after becoming personal astronomer to George III. A tree later fell on the telescope when positioned in his son's garden.

This telescope with its astonishing 4 ft (1.2 m) aperture was made in 1789 at Slough, eight years after William Herschel discovered Uranus at Bath. He lived there first after moving from Germany, initially teaching music and making telescopes with the help of his talented sister, Caroline. She would become renowned for her cataloguing, including those of John Flamsteed's publications, and by herself discovered eight comets. Decorated by the Royal Astronomy Society in 1828, she also found the time to be a gifted singer. The Royal Society awarded their prestigious Copley medals to both her father and brother, John, who would become equally renowned and established an observatory near Capetown in 1834.

Although William Herschel lived to be eighty-four and was described as a 'great, simple, good old man known for his readiness to explain his sublime conceptions of the universe', he would possibly have been more than astonished that, 155 years after his death, the unmanned and identical spaceships *Voyagers 1 and 2*, would be launched in 1977. Taking advantage of a 'line-up' of outer planets that occurs only once every 176 years that would no doubt have greatly interested William Herschel, the two *Voyager* craft were launched to catapult into Saturn's orbit. *Voyager 1* then spun out of the plane of the solar system. *Voyager 2*, moving at 40,000 mph (64,000 kph) then continued on course for a seven year journey to reach Uranus; four times the size of the Earth and covered in clouds of frozen methane. *Voyager 2* then proceeded on to Neptune; a total distance of 4 billion miles (6.5 billion Km).

William Herschel would be given the accolade 'the founder of sidereal astronomy' for his systematic observations of the heavens and is forever attributed with the discovery of Uranus when using a reflecting telescope 7 x 6.5 ft (2 x 1.9 m) and initially called it *Sidus Georgium*. This planet, now named after the Greek sky god, had been observed as a 'fixed star' on quite a few previous occasions much earlier and inevitably by John Flamsteed, who began studying astronomy when ill health forced him to leave the free school in Derby when aged sixteen. Then, after observing a solar eclipse, he began corresponding with astronomers; a few years later his studies came to the attention of the Royal Society and were published. (Ref Finale B)

Mr Harry Johnston, keeper of John Harrison's pendulum clock. Commissioned in 1720 for the new stable block at Brocklesby Park, it is still working today. (Author)

Holy Trinity Church, Barrow upon Humber, where John Harrison was choirmaster (Author)

John Harrison's cottage in Barrow Upon Humber, now sadly demolished (P Cherry)

PART TWO

TELLING TIMES: SUNDIALS TO CAESIUM ATOMS

'The stars move still, time runs, the clock will strike ......'.
                    Christopher Marlowe, 1564-1593, *Faustus.*

Primitive man probably used his own shadow for time-measurement; shade from surrounding trees and rocks would be a seasonal indication for the planting of crops. A simple wooden staff plunged vertically in the ground would also have sufficed. To him, the sun would be moving and not the earth. All that came later, but we still use the terms of the sun 'rising' and 'setting'.

The use of the sky as a clock has never been in any doubt down through the ages. During the century 1400 BC King Akhenaton of Egypt, husband of the beautiful Queen Nefertiti, would strive to abolish the traditional religious cult and replace it with a one-god worship devoted to the very essential sun.

By 1300 BC there is reference on record of the Egyptians having a sundial and by 1000 BC they had improvised their time-keeping with the *merkhet*, a *'shadow clock'* from the *'hour of rising ...... to high rising'* and then progressed to the water clock, the *clepsydra*, indicating hours of equal length from the levels of the water.

A sarcophagus, dated around the 5th century BC, has recently been discovered under the sea at Alexandria and inscribed with hieroglyphics suggesting it is the oldest recorded document on astronomy ever found in Egypt. We do know that by 300 BC King Ptolemy of Egypt had established a library and the first recorded observatory at Alexandria.

Also busily calculating down the centuries were the Mesopatamians, devising the *sexagesima* mathematical series. The renowned Greek astronomer, Hipparchus, lived from 190-120 BC and made the first known accurate catalogue of over 800 stars, calculating their brightness by a system of 'sixes'. He went on to define mathematical rules involving the sides and angles of triangles, otherwise trigonometry, and applied his knowledge of 'spheres' to formulate a table of 'chords'.

Hipparchus then applied his rigorously mathematical standards to determining the location of places on the earth's surface. The circumference of the globe was sectioned lengthwise by 360 divisions; demonstrated by a series of huge circles running through both north and south poles and each known as the 'gradus' or 'step', otherwise 'degree' to us. He then simply put the lengthwise '0.00' degree for east-west reference as a starting point at where he lived, creating the Isle of Rhodes' Meridian.

The north-south 'equator' was more easily defined; just a simple division around the middle of the earth forming the north and south hemispheres. The Babylonians had long discovered that the length of day varies when travelling north. The imaginary lines of *'longi'* and *'lati'* meaning 'broad' plus the suffix *'tude'* meaning 'abstraction' evolved.

The 'parallels' of latitude, when one degree apart on the earth's surface, correspond to 63 miles per degree (100 Km). When the east-west meridians are one degree apart, the distance is calculated as 70 miles (112 Km). Where they cross the parallels of latitude at right angles (ninety degrees), their intersections pinpoint a position and you know exactly where you are on a map or globe.

Various meridians would be established at the map makers' convenience after Hipparchus who would greatly inspire his disciple, Claudius Ptolemy, to devise a series of mathematical tables calculating the measurements of the radius and arcs of the circle in the values of the number 'six'. Thus divisions of the hour or *'hora'*, the Greek word for 'season' would eventually become units of 1/60th for the minute ('), and 1/3600th for the second (''). Around 300 BC the Greeks would give the name of *gnomon* (meaning to *know*) to the rod or *style* of a sundial.

These measurements of 'sixes' would eventually become very commonplace when adopted for display on clock dials to record the passage of time. However, they were initially used to measure distances on the charts and globes used in astronomy and navigation; all points on the north-south equator having a latitude of 0.00 degrees, the arc formed between a point on the 'parallel' of the equator and then stretching to the centre of the earth, forms an angle with the equator.

By the time the north and south poles are reached the arc has become an angle of 90 degrees or quarter of a circle of 360 degrees – the quadrant. Using these methods of calculation and taking the most central point of the earth as 0.00 degrees would emerge the *'sextant'* for measuring an arc 1/6th of the estimated 360 degrees circumference of the earth along the north-south equator

But still by 140 AD the Alexandria-based astronomer Claudius Ptolemy, would persist in believing that the earth was static and the centre of the universe. By measuring the movement of the sun and stars he believed the size of the earth could be established and proceeded to map the planets mathematically. The circumference of planet earth is now assessed at 24,912 miles (40,091 Km).

Each era has its technology and the accurate measurement of time slowly progressed down the centuries. The word 'dial' is a derivation of the Latin *dies*, or day.

The earliest sundials, however, were understandably far from accurate for the gnomon was horizontally placed; the length of days varied considerably north and south of the equator. It was not until the 11th and 12th centuries that the advantages of a sundial with a gnomon parallel to the earth's axis were realised and developed, possibly first in Morocco. These would show equal divisions every 24 hours. Time measurement was becoming increasingly scientifically based.

The earliest vertical sundial in Britain, circa 685 AD, is believed to be that at Bewcastle Cross in Cumbria. By then Europe had survived the Dark Ages. During the following two centuries there were many remarkable innovations as man attempted to control time-measurement mechanically. As we know, there are two essential components needed for this; an energy store in the form of a raised weight or coiled spring, plus an *escapement* or route that regulates the release of energy from that store. The *verge* or *crown wheel* escapement would eventually emerge and control the release of energy by means of an oscillated weighted bar. A system of 'gearing' was also needed to transmit the motion to a hand on a dial which measured each hour in units of 1:60, otherwise the minute.

There is record in the Chinese literature of some form of mechanical clock in the 7th century. In 1172 AD they would document and print the details, probably by letter-set, of their incredible water-balance escapement clock.

The first public mechanical clock know in Europe is probably that attributed to the Dondi father and son team responsible for the time-piece at Carrera Palace in Padua, Italy, in 1344. Two decades later, in 1364, Henri de Vick in France perfected the balance wheel as the *foliot*, or crossbar. The more sophisticated public dials of medieval Europe 'entertained' by using figures mechanically and incorporating bells, carillon, as at Rouen in France – in England at Salisbury in 1386 and a few years later at Wells, Somerset. But for domestic use, the progress of the mechanical clock was impeded by lack of the very precise skills and tools needed until the arrival of the pendulum.

Medieval Europe became familiar with the hour glass, the crushed-eggs and sands-of-time receptacles with their varying apertures, water clocks and the burning of candles. Ordinary people relied on the bell (otherwise the *cloche* or *clocca*) of the nearest monastery, town hall or castle. Until the 13th century these were operated manually and timed by the local sundial, often placed vertically for the convenience of passers-by.

During the 15th century Claudius Ptolemy's tables of the moon's motions had become available to the Polish Nikolas Kopernigk who was studying Greek in Italy prior to a career in theology. He also found the writings of Plato and became friendly with an astronomer. Elizabeth I was ten year's old when Copernicus, as he became known, published his life's work *'De Revolutionibus Orbium Coelestium'* and then discreetly died. Written in six sections during several decades, the discourse explained that the sun was indeed the centre of our universe and the earth spherical and rotating; thus refuting the unbelievers Claudius Ptolemy, Aristotle and many others.

Elizabeth I's father, Henry VIII, had astutely seconded to a fellowship at Corpus Christi College, Oxford, his own personal astronomer and horologist or 'reader of time'. Officially known as the *Deviser of the King's Horologies,* Nicholas Kratzer from Munich would teach the 'doctrine of the spheres'. To us, merely the deductions to be made from the simple, or not so simple, sundial.

As a child Elizabeth I would have been familiar with multiple sundials in which each individual dial served as a component for the whole. They were mainly intended for decorative purposes, often unattached to a building and showed off the skills and prestige of the mathematician. The oldest known of these in England and attributed to Nicholas Kratzer is probably that in the churchyard at Elmley Castle, near the Vale of Evesham in Worcestershire and dated around 1545.

Forty years later, around 1583, when the drum water-clock with its internal intricate divisions for recording time-measurement was known to be 'on the market' in Elizabethan England, a young Italian medical student from a musical background and a keen disciple of Copernicus made a salutary observation in the magnificent cathedral of his affluent home town, Pisa.

For Galileo Galilei noted, and probably timed with his own pulse beat, that when a lamp swung as a pendulum, regardless of the range of swing, almost always the same amount of time was needed to complete the oscillation. The dawn of the age when the time-period of a pendulum swing could be controlled to aid accurate time-measurement had begun. However, the sundial, sand glass and water clock would survive until the 18th century; they were cheap, reasonably accurate and easy to repair.

The 19th century would bring the discovery of the alkali metal caesium by Bunsen and Kirchoff in 1860. The 20th century would find the Bell Telephone Laboratories in 1928 illustrating the *piezoelectric* effect defined 'as the frequency of oscillation controlling the frequency of the mechanical vibrations of the crystal'. The term is derived from the Greek 'piezein' meaning 'to press' and can perhaps be more simply explained as the 'production of electricity by applying a mechanical stress to certain crystals' or conversely 'in which stress is produced in a crystal as a result of an applied voltage'. Whatever, the first quartz crystal clock was soon produced. Six years later the United States Naval Observatory would be utilising a crystal-controlled clock for automatic transmission of time signals.

And just two decades after that the unique properties of caesium atoms to undergo energy transition, when bombarded by very precisely-tuned radio waves, was isolated by two scientists in 1955 at the National Physical Laboratory at Teddington; not far from the Richmond home of Elizabeth I where she died in 1603.

This discovery by Essen and Parry made possible the sophisticated *'atomic time scale'*, unaffected by the earth's wobble and weather and rendering nightly observation of the 'clock stars' obsolete for time-measurement. In 1967 the 13th General Conference of Weights and Measures redefined the 'second' in terms of atomic standards:

'The second (s) is the duration of 9,192, 631,770 periods of the radiation corresponding to the transition between the two hyper-fine levels of the ground state of the cesium-133 atom'.

Further development was carried out in cooperation with the United States Naval Observatory. Small commercial models of atomic clocks weighing around 66 pounds (30 Kg) were subsequently carried on aircraft. A rack of atomic clocks are now continuously monitored at Teddington, providing the National Time and Frequency Service time-measurement to a millionth of a second – or one second per million years. An unbelievable fact to many of us today, but even more so to the pioneers of time-keepers particularly of the 16th and 17th centuries. A gallery in the British Museum is devoted to a collection of meticulously crafted and elaborate clocks and watches of that period; some ingenuously concealed in crucifixes. Although obviously very expensive, they were mostly inaccurate, particularly at sea.

Farther afield, at Hampton Court Palace, purloined by Henry VIII from his Lord Chancellor Cardinal Wolsey during the 1520's, the magnificent astronomical clock brilliantly perfected by Nicholas Oursian probably from the designs of Nicholas Kratzer on the orders of the monarch, can still be seen. It is in the main court, above the second-floor window. The diameter of the dial measures 7 ft 10 in (2.4 m). Constructed in 1540 before the discoveries of Copernicus and Galileo were known, the sun is shown revolving around the earth.

It was intricately designed, with much nicety, to indicate the hour, the month, the day of the month, the number of days since the beginning of the year and the phases of the moon; another feature was the calculation of high water at London Bridge. It lasted for three centuries before the dial needed replacing and a new mechanism made. Yet another hundred years went by, until the 1970's when it was cleaned; the true colours were then revealed and the clock repainted according.

CREATING THE COMPASS

"A needle placed upon a dart is used by sailors to steer by when the Bear is hidden by clouds…"

Alexander Neckham, *De Nominibus Utensilium,* 1180.
(English school teacher and scientist)

By 500 BC it was known to the Greeks that the local black mineral ore, a form of iron oxide, found at Magnesia in Thessaly, Macedonia, had unique attracting and repelling properties; otherwise distinct magnetic 'poles' that could be used as a navigating indicator of the true north. The origin of the compass was, and still is, is shrouded in ancient history and probably of Chinese origin. In the 11th century AD written records tell of a magnetic compass in use on land and also at sea by 'foreign' sailors, probably Muslim, navigating in the China and South Seas between Canton and Sumatra. The compass, derived from the word *compassus* meaning measure, came into being. Nevertheless, the first written evidence in the West is attributed to Alexander Neckham.

Nearly a century after, the *Laws of Magnetism* were formulated by a Dominican friar in 1269, Peter the Pilgrim (alias French Crusader Petrus Peregrinus de Maricourt). He not only wrote of the floating compass, but also manually explored the surface of a sphere with a piece of magnetic iron ore he had painstakingly fashioned as a rudimentary tool. The name 'poles' was given to the areas in which the magnetic power concentrated; he noted that seamen unable to see the sun or stars to steer by would "magnetize a needle with a lodestone and place it through a straw floating on water and when it came to rest it was pointing at the Pole Star". The 'lodestone' being the piece of magnetic iron ore used for 'loading' onto the improvised compass needle often made of wood or natural fibre.

The readings would later be transcribed onto the now familiar 'rosecard' with its thirty-two divisions, derived from the national emblem of England. This would prove invaluable not only for assessing the divisions of the horizon as compass readings, but later also for the precise identification and recording of wind direction.

In 1873 it is on record that the indefatigable William Thomson, later Baron Kelvin of Largs, undertook to write a series of articles on the mariner's compass. This would proved to be the catalyst whereby he 'overhauled' the compass as it then was. Among the many innovations he introduced was a reduction by around 6% of the weight of the 10 in card (4 cm) while increasing the time of the needle swing. He also achieved compensation for the magnetic deviation caused by the steel construction of ships and invented sounding apparatus. The Thomson tide gauge, tidal harmonic analyzer and tide predictor became essential tools of navigation.

In the 20th century, aircraft and large vessels would progress to using the gyrocompass, which, as its name suggests, utilises the effect of the Earth's rotation on a spinning object's axis of rotation.

ROGER BACON – MAGNIFYING GLASS

For any man with half an eye,
What stands before him may espy;
But optics sharp it needs I ween,
To see what is not to be seen.

(John Trumball, USA, mid 18th/19th century.)

Lenses, with their unique capacity to deflect light and converge rays to a focus, were apparently originally so-named because of their resemblance to the convex-shaped seeds of the humble lentil vegetable. In 1268 the west-of-England born and outspoken philosopher, Roger Bacon, noted the use of optical lenses for reading in Europe and swiftly realised the potential of the simple magnifying glass. He was a brilliant experimental scientist who unsuccessfully campaigned for the 'the secrets of nature by positive study' to be included in the curriculum of the universities.

A few decades earlier the possibility of an optical instrument to magnify distant objects, the 'telescope', had already been considered; single lenses for personal use would be first noted on a portrait circa 1352 at Treviso, Italy. Eyeglasses were also recorded in a portrait of St Jerome in 1480; he was later adopted as patron saint of spectacle-makers. The Italian Renaissance artist and architect, Raphael, painting in 1517, shows Pope Leo X with concave lenses; the first indication of them. Until then, only convex lenses have been recorded for age-related conditions.

Just over two and a half centuries later, in 1784, the Boston-born printer and brilliantly versatile author, scientist and diplomat Benjamin Franklin invented bifocal lenses; as well as lightning conductors and much else. His father, a maker of soap and candles, had emigrated from Banbury in Oxfordshire. In 1827 and a few years before he was appointed Royal Astronomer, Sir George Biddell Airy perfected a cylindrical lens to correct his astigmatism; a condition only really recognised and documented in 1864.

Lenses were originally made of transparent quartz and beryl but 'optical glass' would be pioneered in Venice and Nuremberg, paving the way for the emergence of microscopes around 1590. However, the *Laws of Refraction*, dealing with the concept of light bending and changing speed when passing through glass, would not be drawn up until the mid-17th century. Until recently it has been considered that the first refracting telescope, whereby light was encouraged to fall onto a converging long-focus lens and the image magnified by a short-focus eyepiece, was made by the spectacle-maker Hans Lippershey in Holland in 1608.

Apparently, he accidentally noted that two lenses, when held at a distance from each other but both focusing on the same object, greatly enlarged that object; in fact, his church steeple. Hans Lippershey then reputedly put the two lenses, at the same relative distance apart, within a tube.

However, the concept of vision magnified practically from a distance is also attributed to two other spectacle-makers in Holland around that time. Notwithstanding, there is now evidence that a telescopic device was considered some three decades earlier by the 16th century London instrument maker and authority on navigation, Leonard Digges, working together with his son, but possibly the invention was considered too valuable for military purposes to be made generally known. Thomas Digges was considered one of the three leading mathematicians in England by Tycho Brahe; the esteemed Danish astronomer who would later move to Prague and teach Johannes Kepler.

Whatever and whenever the origins of the telescope with its two lenses, the business of telescope-making swiftly became very popular for both amateur and professional.

Microscopes also came on the market. First a *compound* model invented by Dutch spectacle-maker Zacharius Janssen, contemporary of Hans Lippershey, then a *simple* model with one lens, in 1677. The latter would be further developed by Kepler, Scheiner, Huygen and Wenham, and many others down the centuries.

The *Laws of Reflection* had been expounded as far back as 300 BC when the Greek mathematician, Euclid, was so much intrigued with spaces and shapes that he formulated 'geometry' and wrote his book *Elements*. Nearly two thousand years later, the Scottish mathematician and astronomer, James Gregory, published the *Optica promota* in 1663 describing a reflecting telescope using two mirrors to gather light, rather than the lens system of the refracting telescope; apparently during his short lifetime it was difficult to get the glass ground precisely enough to complete it. Five years later, the first successful reflecting telescope would be made by Isaac Newton; light being transferred from a concave mirror of long focal length via a secondary optical mechanism to finally reflect onto a short-focus eyepiece. It was 9 inches long (23 cm) and the mirror 2 inches in diameter (5 cm). Presented to the Royal Society by its maker, it remains a prized possession.

In 1672, Cassegrain built a reflecting telescope using a convex, instead of a concave, mirror. Fifty years later, John Hadley, inventor of the sextant, improved on the Newtonian telescope with a metallic speculum of 6 inch aperture (15 cm) and almost 63 inch focal length (160 cm); he also improved on the Gregorian design in 1726. William Herschel also greatly advanced the art of making mirrors for reflecting telescopes by using a speculum-metal composed of a hard brittle alloy, consisting of one part tin and two parts copper, with the ability to reflect 60%.

William Parsons, otherwise Lord Rosse and an ardent astronomer, painstakingly experimented with solid specula composed of copper and tin. He built a series of telescopes at his castle in Ireland resulting in 1845 with the giant reflecting Leviathan of Parsonstown containing a 72 inch mirror (183 cms) attached to a 56 ft tube (17 m). He then discovered the first spiral galaxy, M51, and three years later named the

Crab Nebula. The Royal Society and Dublin University duly honoured him. Until then, the time-honoured method for perfecting a lens was that of onerously grinding with emery grains and finally precisely shaping with optician's rouge. However, the concave-curved structure of the telescope-mirrored lens, reflecting the light rays to a focus and composed of the speculum-metal combination of copper and tin, required frequent repolishing for it tarnished rapidly.

The difficulties of finding an alternative process were considerable. A reflecting coating had to be on the front of the glass to prevent loss of light. The method long-used for making the familiar domestic mirror, with its tin and mercury backing, was therefore not suitable for the development of a telescope reflecting lens. Thus, during the early 18th century the refracting telescope returned to enjoy short periods of popularity. By 1733, Chester Moor Hall of Essex was the first person to succeed in making achromatic refracting telescopes; that is, showing objects free from colour.

He did this by combining lenses of different kinds of glass, nullifying colours by their different refractive properties; having deduced that the human eye being composed of different humours successfully manages to refract black and white images on the retina. However, the development of the achromatic refractor telescope is due to the efforts of one John Dolland who invented it independently of Chester Moor Hall, taking out the patent in 1758. His son, Peter, would improve on the original design in 1765; introducing a model consisting of two convex lenses of crown glass, interspersed with a concave lens of flint glass. The casting of glass disks for large lenses was improved, notably by the German optician and physicist Joseph von Fraunhofer. As well as supplying large lenses for refracting telescopes he also used his expertise to study the dark lines in the sun's spectrum; these still bear his name.

Later, in the USA, optician Alvan Clark of Boston would also be successful in pioneering the manufacture of optical disks of great size. In 1862 he tested an 18.5-inch (47 cm) refracting telescope made for the Dearborn Observatory. Using the brightest star in the sky, the Sirius or Dog Star, for reference, he was the first observer to record the appearance of it revolving together with a 'companion' star; an occurrence only seen every fifty years. His firm would later supply a 36-inch lens (91 cm) to the Lick Observatory on Mount Hamilton, California in 1888 and a 40-inch lens (102 cm) to Yerkes Observatory, Williams Bay, Wisconsin in 1897.

The complication of these large refracting lenses was, and is, that the object glass is only supported by the circumference and can sag under their own weight; apart from other anomalies connected to the condition of the glass itself that are inherent or may develop. This problem would be solved by the experiment of the renowned German organic chemist Baron Justus von Liebig, demonstrating around 1849 that a thin layer of silver could be deposited on glass. This made possible the future successful development of the reflecting telescope in preference to the refracting variety.

The French physicist, John Léon Foucault applied the silver-on-glass process to the testing and making of mirrors. In 1856 Karl August von Steinheil of Munich developed a process of consecutively coating glass telescope disks with reflecting films of silver; when tarnished these could be easily removed with acid and speedily replaced with new layers of brilliant silver. During the 1930s, coating with aluminium was pioneered successfully to create a hard and durable reflecting film with a shelf-life of five to ten years, in contrast to the silver coatings which lasted only a few months.

GALILEO – TESTING TIMES FOR PENDULUMS AND POPES

"The Bible shows us the way to go to Heaven but not the way the Heavens go."

(Galileo's lament when respectfully confined to house arrest in 1662 after being considered by some to be more dangerous than Luther and Calvin.)

Galilei Galileo soon learned of the development in Holland of the refracting telescope. He immediately made one for himself, using a convex object lens and concave eyepiece in a leaden tube and swiftly presented it on completion, plus a few refinements, to the Doge of Venice in 1609. We are told the Senate upgraded his lectureship at Padua University to a lifetime contract and doubled his salary. Galileo would experiment with telescopes all his life, forever devising methods for checking the curvature of the glass lenses. But within a year of perfecting his first instrument he improved the magnifying power by more than ten times that of its original threefold capacity. Then, as we all know, in 1610 he looked up into the night sky with it.

How some of those astute stargazers of ancient civilizations would have enjoyed being at his elbow! Not for those discerning peoples any nonsense about a flat Earth; that it was spherical had long been realised. Maybe they just deduced that if everything observed in the sky was round perhaps we might simply be round, too? Their knowledge was handed down the generations and along the great trade routes of Asia and Arabia. In the world of Galileo the possibility of drifting clouds of gases and dust orbiting the sun and being pulled into clumps and accruing, held together by gravity in a solar system for millions of years, was probably as beyond comprehension as the achievement of our present 'space age' a few generations ago.

Galileo would have been even more astounded to know that three centuries after he first looked up into the sky with his sophisticated telescope, the spacecraft *Voyager 1* and *Voyager 2* would travel for two years to reach Jupiter in 1979; the astonishing photographs taken by their electronic cameras beamed back to Earth via the large white dishes attached. And he would probably be even more delighted to know that another spacecraft, *Galileo*, was carried into orbit by one of the four space shuttles, *Atlantis*, in 1989. Passing Venus and two satellites it began orbiting Jupiter in 1995 on an extended and extensive survey.

The human Galileo, however, fell from grace. His deductions were eventually considered by the church authorities running the universities as too upsetting for the status quo. Although there was much support for his findings in certain quarters, nevertheless the belief that divine authority must not be challenged held sway. Having suitably recanted some of his supposed errors of observation to the satisfaction of the Inquisition without undue pressure, the papal authorities spared him prison. Galileo was allowed to return to his home outside Florence for what would be the last eight years of his life.

At first, avidly observing the daily and monthly motions of the moon and latterly vigorously thinking, experimenting, discoursing to his disciples and confiding in his very intelligent daughter. Although blind by 1638 he published his most valuable work, the *Dialogue on Two New Sciences*, in Holland. The following year and a long way away at Hoole in Lancashire, a young astronomer, the Reverend Jeremiah Horrocks, calculated that a transit of Venus would occur on Sunday 24 November, 1639. Somehow, apparently, this date had not appeared in the star almanacs then in use; a popular one was compiled by the German-born Johannes Kepler, who improved on Galileo's design of telescope by using a convex eyepiece which considerably improved the field of vision. He also defined light rays and proved that planets follow elliptical orbits around the sun. A Protestant, he was obliged to live in Prague and eventually Silesia.

Jeremiah Horrocks observed the transit from his attic-telescope between church services and predicted recurrence. The future master mariner, James Cook, born in the neighbouring county of Yorkshire nearly a century later, would be despatched to Tahiti to view. An event unknown to Galileo, who died of a fever in 1642 on his small estate at Arcetri, aged seventy-eight, pondering on the application of the pendulum to time-measurement as England began seven bitter years of civil war. On Christmas Day that year, three months after his father's death, Isaac Newton would be born at Woolsthorpe Manor, near Grantham in Lincolnshire. We can visit there today, courtesy of the National Trust.

Oliver Cromwell began his rule as Lord Protector in 1649 as Galileo's son, Vincenzio, produced the 'Proposed Pendulum Application', made to his father's design and representing the first known attempt to utilise a pendulum to control the rate of a weight or spring-driven clock. By 1657, in Holland, the renowned mathematician, astronomer and physicist Christiaan Huygens, having considerably adapted the Keplerian telescope, much improved his capacity for celestial observations. Inspired by his need to measure time exactly, he perfected a 'Pendulum Timepiece'.

His work on the length of a pendulum, and the time of its oscillation, led to the theory of centrifugal force in circular motion. This would one day greatly influence Isaac Newton's theories on gravity as a mechanical agent, and also cause John Harrison considerable concern when on a sea-trial with his first mechanical non-pendulum clock. Huygens, who had himself unsuccessfully experimented with several pendulum timepieces at sea, would be justifiably greatly honoured in learned circles for his work on the development of physical optics and the revolutionary wave theory of light. He made and presented a 123 ft (37 m) telescope to the Royal Society in London. The Vatican formally recognised the teachings of Galileo in 1992, absolving him from heresy three hundred and fifty years after his death.

ALL AT SEA WITHOUT LONGITUDE

"But for God's almighty providence and the wideness of the sea…"

(Diarist Samuel Pepys, the Admiralty's first-ever real administrator, expressing his serious concerns of the perils of navigation before he died in 1703.)

In 1714, the Longitude Act was passed by a Parliament much concerned with the lack of safety at sea, caused by mariners still losing their direction; perhaps with only a little latitude to rely on. Samuel Pepys was only too well aware of this grievous situation as it was his job to supply the Navy with ships and knew at first hand the losses suffered.

The government of the day's decision was prompted by several major disasters and especially that occurring in 1707, when a fleet of British warships with their flagship foundered on the Gilstone Rocks, off the Scilly Isles; over two thousand sailors perished. Among them Admiral Sir Cloudesley Shovell; his memorial in Westminster Abbey was carved by Grinling Gibbons, working unusually in marble.

The Board of Longitude was established and 'A Public Reward' offered, comprising a series of prizes, the major one valued at £20,000, to be awarded for a method determining longitude at sea to within half a degree. Although the Royal Observatory Greenwich had been active for several decades and its hard-pressed assistants manually computing masses of observations every year, by the turn of the 18th century the problem of longitude remained unsolved. The only solution then still considered seriously viable by 'the great and good' was that of the lunar method; measuring the time travelled between the fixed stars as the surest way of deciding an east-west position at sea.

Since ancient times an east-west positioning on land had been achieved, initially by observing the altitudes of the sun between important landmarks, then using the 'marching distances' between to estimate time travelled.

It is on record that in 250 BC the Greek mathematician,

Eratosthenes, had observed that when in southern Egypt at Syene, the sun was vertically overhead at noon during the summer solstice; then it is furthest from the equator and appears to pause, but deviated by about seven degrees at Alexandria in the north at the same time of day. A line of longitude represented by an arc could thus be drawn between the two places.

For many, many centuries a daily reckoning system had been in existence; beginning at noon when the sun was nearest with its shadow on land the shortest, the days and nights would be measured in derivates of 'six'. Twelve divisions for each day and night came into usage. The smaller divisions of the 'minute' evolved.

Then the 'second', or 'next after the first', calculation; this was well nigh impossible without an accurate reference point. This would eventually only be achieved with the discoveries of the almost exact speed of the Earth's rotation and the oscillations of the pendulum as standard measures.

Until uniform time-measurement could be accurately established globally, the use of the sun as a very necessary scientific instrument would remain until the early 20th century. Clocks and watches would be set by the sundial, either public or in the garden.

Strange and puzzling ancient stone circles, possibly proclaiming the seasons by mirroring the height of the sun, can still be seen on our landscape, having somehow been put there by mysterious design and unexplained feats of labours. Those Henges were in existence by 3500 BC, around the same time as evidence of the wheel in southern Mesopotamia, where the 'sexagesimal' system of counting in sixes evolved.

Down the centuries, however, the telling of the accurate time at sea remained a mystery that could only be solved by infallible, rigorously documented and quickly deducible lunar calculations. Or by the miracle of a reliable sea-going 'impossible' clock unaffected by deviating temperatures, humidity, atmospheric pressure variations, gravity and the rocking of ships on the oceans.

Both options remained unavailable until the 'battle for longitude' was eventually won in the late 18th century. First, theoretically and slowly with the *Nautical Almanac* then, speedily and practically, with John Harrison's invention of a successful sea-going clock; establishing the science of marine chronometry.

Safety at sea was further helped in 1809 when Francis Beaufort invented the 'wind scale force'. In 1854, Vice-Admiral Robert Fitzroy, who had earlier commanded *HMS Beagle* with Charles Darwin and twenty-two chronometers aboard plus a brief to accurately rechart the South American coast, was appointed to lead the newly-formed Meteorology Department.

By the end of the 1850s, an organised network of meteorological stations was established. Robert Fitzroy was also a pioneer of the Lifeboat Association; *HMS Beagle* had very nearly capsized on her first voyage. He published his acclaimed *Weatherbook* in 1863.

However, the daily appearance of the sun remained helpful to navigators. Apart from providing morale-boosting warmth and good cheer, accurate local time still needed to be known aboard; to compare with the GMT registered on the chronometers in order to calculate the distances travelled.

As we know, the Earth is almost 25,000 miles (41,000 Km) in circumference; each degree of longitude measured at its axis corresponds to around 69 miles (111 Km) along the equator. As the lines of longitude converge at the poles, their degree measurements have decreased proportionally at a regular rate.

Further milestones would be the application of the electric telegraph system begun in the late 1830s; then the invention of the Morse Code system of communication the following decade. The substitution of dots and dashes, representing letters of the alphabet, would miraculously transcend language barriers in conveying GMT worldwide along the first submarine cables.

Even more miraculously would be the development of radio-telegraphy allowing transmission of the human voice beyond the horizon, heralding in live communication between ship and shore. No matter then that the sun, always shrouded in celestial mystery, was behind the clouds! The ability to immediately notify distress at sea with the universally understood 'SOS', the Mayday call, would save countless lives.

JOHN HARRISON – THE TRIALS OF CLOCKING TIME AT SEA

"Hide not your talents
They for use were made,
What's a sundial in the shade."

Benjamin Franklin (Founder, American Philosophical Society, 1743.)

John Harrison, the Lincolnshire village wood-carver and self-taught clockmaker with a love of music, was born in 1693. Four years later his family went to live on the south bank of the River Humber; a ferry crossing away from the Yorkshire port of Hull. There, in adulthood, he would easily have come into contact with sailors and fully appreciated that as the Earth turns fifteen degrees every hour, an error in a clock of just one minute could put a ship dangerously off course. The rewards being offered then by the Board of Longitude, apart from the top prize of £20,000, also included sums of £15,000 and £10,000 for finding a solution for longitude to within two-thirds of a degree and one degree respectively.

These very large cash inducements provoked a great response; some supposed solutions were very farcical but none were of any significance. In 1730, the answer to the longitude problem was still felt to be in the 'heavens above', when choirmaster John Harrison decided the time was right to make his first journey to London and seek further advice about his ideas for a sea-going clock. Finding his way up to the Royal Observatory Greenwich he called on the Royal Astronomer Edmund Halley who by then, it is recorded, was beginning to despair of ever having the Lunar Tables completed.

John Harrison had with him the illustrated designs of his 'gridiron pendulum' which was so uniquely constructed that it did not vary with temperature; proved in his small cottage home by leaving some clocks in the cold and others in a room banked up with fires during freezing winters! Always an experimenter, he had learned his craft working at home; initially experimenting with clocks made of oak and innovatively and logically incorporating workings made of a wood from the Caribbean, 'lignum vitae' (*Guaiacum Officinale*). As the name implies, the natural resins of this timber never dry out, making it an essential component for effortlessly reducing friction; frequent oiling of a clock mechanism is not required. Together with his brother, James, a revolutionary turret clock needing no lubrication was made for the stable block at neighbouring Brocklesby Park; the estate of Sir Charles Pelham at Yarborough in Lincolnshire. It is still there in use today. (Ref Tips for Tourists)

Even more remarkably, Harrison had learned to set his clocks to the time of the movement of the non-revolving 'fixed stars', from the west side of a neighbour's chimney to the east side of his window frame. He calculated with remarkable accuracy the timing of the stars as they appeared, earlier every evening by three minutes and 54 seconds.

As is now well known, Royal Astronomer Edmund Halley was impressed with Harrison's knowledge and designs, but not having sufficient expertise to advise further, directed him back down to London to see George Graham, the leading clock-maker of day. He was soon greatly impressed with what his visitor had to say and show him. Dining with Harrison he encouraged him to continue the work; helping with the offer of a substantial personal loan.

A few years after, in 1736, Harrison sailed to Lisbon on the *Centurion* taking his first clock, H1, on a sea-going trial. He was away five weeks and often very seasick, returning on the *Orford*. It is on record that the captain of the *Centurion* found his guest to be sober, honest, very industrious and modest; but considered that the difficulties he was encountering on the task might make all his efforts impossible.

The prototype H1 was portable, rather unwieldy and designed similarly to his wooden clocks. It stood 2 ft high (63 cms), weighed 75 pounds (34 Kg) and was very effective but not quite good enough. In order to offset motion at sea, the function of a pendulum was substituted by rocking balance arms joined with springs; some of the workings were made of wood. Its potential, however, was recognised both by scientists and the Board of Longitude, which awarded Harrison some of the prize money.

He moved to London and proceeded to make H2; standing 2.5 ft high (76 cms) with a weight of 85 pounds (39 Kg). This was made mostly of brass with a *remontoir* rewinding every 3.75 minutes. But still Harrison was not satisfied and there was no further sea trial. He spent another 19 years, until 1754, perfecting H3, which stood 2 ft high (59 cms), weighed 80 pounds (43 Kg) and with a *remontoir* capable of rewinding every thirty seconds. Despite incorporating some brilliant revolutionary ideas including the 'caged roller race' for "my curious third machine..." as he described it, nevertheless the accuracy he needed constantly eluded him. For a sea-going clock needed to be accurate to six seconds a day, in order to comply with the Board of Longitude's requirement that a ship's longitude must be within thirty nautical miles at the end of a six-week voyage. Harrison had still to wrestle with the problem of centrifugal force, which he had grown to recognise during sailing manoeuvres on the *Centurion*. The Board of Longitude, recognising the inherent ingenuity of his clock-making, continued down the years with some financial support, but John Harrison never went to sea again with H1 or its successors.

Tragically, some years after his trial aboard with H1, the *Centurion* lost her way at sea and many of her crew perished; grievously stricken with scurvy during a long and terrible voyage in a vessel vainly traversing the oceans in a search for land. It is now considered probable that having the model H1 aboard might have saved the *Centurion* from this plight; the sorrow of the occasion was not lost on John Harrison, who had kept in touch with some of the crew.

Around this time he also made his famous 'Regulator' or scientific clock, to supersede his wooden precision clocks. In 1749 he was awarded the Royal Society's highest honour, the gold Copley Medal.

Then, inspired by his new pocket watch, 'the penny dropped' and simply jettisoning thirty years of clock-making John Harrison put all his know-how into perfecting the design of the unique H4.

It was the first balance-wheel timekeeper to have temperature compensation. The unique 'isochronal verge' escapement using smoothly polished diamonds reduced friction to a minimum; each swing of the heavy balance, whether large or small, was thus able to record the same time-measurement. The *remontoir* operated at eight seconds a minute, ensuring constant power. In 1761 his son, William, took to the high seas with H4 for a trial aboard the *Deptford*, destined for Bridgetown in the West Indies. On arrival, waiting to monitor results was arch rival the Reverend Nevil Maskelyne and future Royal Astronomer; staunch advocate of the lunar method and man-of-the-moment.

He was busy compiling more celestial observations for the lunar-distance method still very much favoured. It was only a few years until he would publish the first *Nautical Almanac* and feelings, not always pleasant, ran high! Although, theoretically, longitude should be able to be established by the constancy of the stellar movements, John Harrison was somewhat sceptical of the lunar method enthusiasts.

Brilliantly his invention H4 passed the test; only five seconds lost in 81 days at sea!

Unfortunately, lack of confidence by the Board of Longitude prevented credence being given to the small timepiece presented before it as being the long-awaited solution to the vexed problem of accurate timekeeping at sea. Composed mainly of astronomers and Admiralty officials, the Board could not believe that such an object, weighing only 3 pounds (1.5 Kg) even with its heavy balance wheel, could be both independent of the motion of a ship and accommodate only five to ten seconds per day. The accolade that it was "the forerunner of all precision watches and probably the most important timekeeper ever made..." had yet to come.

H4 was, after all, completely alien in design and appearance to Harrison's previous models; technology in the latter half of the 18th century still proceeded slowly. The Industrial Revolution and the prodigiously inventive efforts of the Victorians were still to come. The Board of Longitude rearranged the terms of reference of their prize to include more trials. Harrison's prodigious attempts for recognition after he had proved H4 successful are every bit as fascinating as his labours in making it.

There were many meetings and arguments with the Board of Longitude who unconditionally wanted his designs at this stage without paying him further; both parties on occasions being very brusque with each other.

Crippled by elementary technicalities and profuse suspicion, there was such dissention that the remainder of the prize money would be persistently refused by the Board. It did, however, retain H4 after demanding that its workings be disclosed formally to them, fearing its secrets might be solved abroad. In all, about £8,000 was still owing John Harrison when his precious creations, H1, H2 and H3 were 'collected' from his house in Red Lion Square by the dreaded Nevil Maskelyne and transferred to the Royal Observatory Greenwich. They remained there, ignominiously out of his reach forever.

H4 was copied by the foremost London watchmakers, Larcum Kendal. The Board of Longitude footed the bill of £500 and K1 went sailing with Captain Cook. Still without his reward, John Harrison and his son stayed at home, made a similar model of the original, named it H5, and petitioned unsuccessfully for their dues. Then, in desperation, they appealed personally to George III who is reputed to have listened and then said "By God, Harrison, I will see you righted!" And he did. H5 was put in the king's personal observatory at Kew and not found wanting. The later tragically-afflicted George III was greatly interested in science himself. His former Timekeeper at Kew, Benjamin Valliamy, had made him a clock fitted with John Harrison's revolutionary 'grasshopper' escapement.

The intransigent Board of Longitude insisted on yet another official trial, but parliamentary intervention ensued. Royal Assent allowed John Harrison to achieve not only the remainder of the prize money, when aged 80 and just three years before his death in 1776, but more importantly to him the recognition of his lifetime's work. Three hundred years after his birth, in 1993, the Harrison Gallery was opened in Flamsteed House at the Royal Observatory Greenwich, containing his incomparable time pieces H1 – H5.

Of John Harrison's long case eight-day clocks, three are still known; one inscribed with his name and village, dated 1715, is now at the Science Museum, Kensington. It is usually on the ground floor in the Modern World Gallery, but exhibits can be moved around.

Also, in the Time Measurement Gallery upstairs in the Science Museum, there may be on view splendid large photographs of John Harrison's masterpieces including one of the meticulously crafted interior of H4 plus some artefacts of the work of Galileo and Huygens.

Nearby may be seen Dondi's Astrarium, devised by the esteemed Italian clock-maker around 1381 to incorporate 'movable feast days' based on Easter and the Astronomical Clock, made for Charles II, showing the high tides at London Bridge.

Usually exhibited and still striking quarter-hourly, echoing with tremendous resonance around the gallery, is the original magnificent clock mechanism instituted in 1392 at Wells Cathedral, Somerset, while nearby the exposed 'innards' of a great turret clock, with its conglomerations of wheels and chains constructed for driving the dials of public clock, leave the visitor in no doubt as to how 'tick-tocking' once occurred.

Next door to the Science Museum, in the Earth Sciences Gallery of the Natural History Museum, also conveniently entered from Exhibition Road, you can ride high by escalator through the centre of a revolving, tumultuous and 'virtual reality' Planet Earth. You might be forgiven for thinking Copernicus and Galileo might also enjoy the experience, accompanied by their suitably humble unbelievers.

Meanwhile, the sceptics of John Harrison might be interested to know that the primary school at Barrow upon Humber now bears not only his name but also a proud and distinctive plaque denoting H4 encircling a globe, on the outside wall. This is clearly visible from the main road while aloft, a splendid weather vane of a similar design plus a ship, sets sail into the clouds.

A splendid replica of a sundial made by his brother, James, is kept inside the parish church of Holy Trinity for safety*; the stone plinth it once rested on can be found on the grass by the south front, a short distance from the cross commemorating the considerable sacrifices suffered by John Harrison's once small village during the wars of the 20th century.

The High Street wends from the church down to the market place with its old stone stocks and bus shelter. Opposite, near the post-office, the side entrance of the Royal Oak tavern leads into a parking area; the site of the rear of John Harrison's former workshop not far from his former home in nearby Barton Lane, so lamentably destroyed

One local resident is now concerned with recreating his cottage for posterity by means of *sgriffto* imaging, contrived from old photographs, on small stone tiles for possible purchase. Another 'amateur' artist will provide paintings. The local WEA published, in 1999, their researches in *John Harrison's Village*. A few miles away at Brocklesby Park, the turret clock continues to attract visitors from all over the world. (ref Finale and Tips for Tourists).

---

* This can be viewed by appointment. The original is cared for at Greenwich.

MICHAEL FARADAY – ELECTRIFYING MAGNETISM

> "*A force could not be communicated between bodies other by some tangible means such as pressure or impact.*"
>
> (From *De Magnete, magneticisque corporibus et...* published 1600 by William Gilbert, Tudor scientist and physician to Elizabeth I.)

In 1600, three years before Elizabeth I died, William Gilbert published his monumental treatise expounding his many years of research using the strictest scientific methods known in his day. Meticulously experimenting, he had particularly concentrated on investigating electrical attractions, magnets and magnetic bodies. He coined the term 'electricity', derived from *Elektron*, the Greek name for amber. By then, nearly two thousand years had elapsed since Thales of Miletus, now referred to as the first of the Greek speculative scientists, recorded that the opaque yellow fossil resin could be activated by simple friction with straw; a phenomena we know as static electricity, otherwise 'free' electrons.

The ancient Greeks were no strangers to magnetism, either. Plato writing in the *Ion*, a name derived from the verb *eimi* meaning 'go', recorded his mentor, Socrates, describing the power of magnetic attraction to support a chain of iron rings one above the other. The later publication of the *De rerum natura* by the Roman poet and philosopher, Titus Lucretius, around 95-52 BC, again noted the power of the local ore at Magnesia in Thessaly, Greece, to attract iron.

From his many observations with magnets, William Gilbert described the 'magnetic poles' and considered the Earth a large magnet; convinced that this theory explained not only the direction of a magnetic needle north and south, but also the dipping and inclination of that needle. He, like Aristotle, remained convinced that that there was no other unseen 'force'. However, the flowing of the 'small particles' or electrons, otherwise electricity, would continue to be very assiduously studied by many people, alongside the mysteries of magnetism. Although the discovery of the actual existence of the electron would not be until 1897 by the English physicist, Joseph J Thomson, from the late 18th century onwards there were many remarkable discoveries.

Positive and negative charges of electricity were identified; the magnitude of the charge always the same and subsequently explained as the "property of certain elementary particles that causes them to undergo electromagnetic interactions." The French physicist, Charles de Coulomb, also developed laws for magnetic poles. The names of the other early pioneers are now absorbed into everyday language, for the efforts of Galvani, Volta, Coulomb, Ampère and Ohm would lay the foundations for the practical achievements of Faraday; later to be theoretically proven principally by Maxwell and Hertz. The mechanical energy needed to revolutionize the world was made possible by the controlled powers of electricity and magnetism. The electric motor and generator came on the scene; electromagnets would be used in electric bells, telephone receivers, radio and TV speakers and tape recorders. Their use in research made possible the exploring of the universe and the speed of the technological revolution.

The kick-start took place in 1791; the same year in which Michael Faraday was born. Then, in Bologna, the Italian anatomist and physiologist Luigi Galvani, famously made known his observation of the twitching of the muscles of a frog's legs when brought into simultaneous contact with two metal wires. What had not been immediately realised, however, was that it was the touching of two wires of different metals, copper and zinc, that made the electricity flow. The movement of the frog's limbs had nothing to do with the concept of 'innate animal electricity' in which Galvani then believed. He had, in fact, induced an electric current which would later be defined as "the direct, or continuous, flow of current along an electrical conductor by bringing dissimilar metals into contact with a moist substance."

Already, some twenty years previously in 1769, Galvani's friend, the Italian physicist Alessandro Volta, had published his first scientific work in 1769; the *De vi attractiva ignis electrici*. In 1775 he invented 'electrophorus', a method to accumulate electric charge. In 1792, a year after Galvani's experience, Alessandro Volta proceeded to investigate electricity in contact with metals. In 1800 he produced the 'Voltaic pile', otherwise the first practical battery which provided the first source of continuous current and laid down the principle of the 'modern' battery; until then some form of gold-plating had been known in early civilisations.

Volta's invention was a brilliantly innovative series of cells constructed with a disc of silver as an 'electrode' with subsequent discs of copper; plus a salt solution, otherwise the 'electrolyte'. A store of electrical energy could thus be built up from an electric current associated with chemical action. In 1794 Volta would be awarded the Copley medal of the Royal Society, one of many honours.

The beginning of the 19th century was 'charged' with the discoveries surrounding the phenomenon of electricity. The anode and cathode, the positive and negative electrodes respectively, were developed. The 'amp' arrived as a measure of electrical current supplied by one 'volt' through 'one ohm'. The Ampère current is calculated as carrying 6.24×10^{23} electrons past any point, or electrode, to another point or electrode, every second. A unit of electric charge, the quantity of electricity transferred by a current of one ampere per second, would come down to us as the 'coulomb'.

A French physicist, André Ampère, would spend the next twenty-five years investigating Volta's achievement and would demonstrate that current-carrying wires exert a force on each other. He introduced the important distinctions between both electrostatics and electric current and between current and voltage. The German physicist, Georg Ohm**,** in 1827 deduced that a current flowing through wire had resistance, and invented the 'ohmmeter' to measure this. Ohm's Law came into existence as $E = IR$, where E = voltage, I = current and R = resistance of current.

The chemical decomposition of a substance by passing an electric current through it was known; the laws concerning 'electrolysis' would later be defined in 1833 by Michael Faraday, the remarkable son of a Yorkshire blacksmith who had migrated south to London in search of work. The nationwide decline of the village forge had begun with the advent of machines capable of superseding the pulling power of horses. The term 'horsepower' as a unit of energy was devised by the former Glasgow instrument maker and engineer, James Watt, of steam-engine fame. The metric unit of electrical power would one day be named after him; defined as the "rate of working in circuit when electromotive force is one volt and intensity of current one ampere".

The achievements of Michael Faraday are now recorded on a plaque along Newington Butts near the Elephant and Castle in south London. He was born nearby when it was still a country district and his first job, after a stint selling newspapers, was working as a bookbinder's apprentice near Baker Street. This, uniquely, gave him unqualified access to the latest scientific publications of the day. Always supported by an encouraging and deeply religious family, he read and studied avidly. A customer would one day give him a ticket for a fee-paying and experimental demonstration, to be given by the renowned chemist Sir Humphrey Davy at the Royal Institution, Albemarle Street, in central London. These lectures were delivered with great aplomb and occasioned considerable excitement scientifically; they were also very popular socially with ladies.

The eager young Michael Faraday listened spellbound. He carefully wrote up the notes of the lecture and bound them; presenting the book to Sir Humphrey Davy and pleading for a job. Eventually, in 1812, when a vacancy unexpectedly occurred he was employed; overjoyed, in the menial position of 'lab boy' to wash up and copy notes. He was twenty-one years old. Sir Humphrey Davy officially retired from the Royal Institution that year, but retained the rank of Honorary Professor. However, he would be sufficiently impressed with Michael Faraday to take him as his assistant on a tour of Europe during 1813-15.

On return, the Cornish-born Sir Humphrey was requested to research conditions in mines to prevent the explosion of mixtures of firedamp and air. The result was the invention of the famous miner's safety lamp that bears his name. His health suffered due to overwork and he went to live in Italy, later dying in Geneva in 1829. Much acclaimed in life and death, among Sir Humphrey's many other achievements was that of the electrolysis of molten salts; resulting in the subsequent isolation of many new metallic elements, particularly sodium and potassium.

Michael Faraday's first years at the Royal Institution were particularly concerned with physical chemistry. He would later liquefy chlorine, isolate benzene and develop electrolysis. But it would be his experiments in 1821, following the observation of Danish physicist Hans Christiaan Oersted noting the previous year that a wire conveying an electric current deflected a pivoted magnetic needle to which it ran parallel, that would bring Michael Faraday fame.

Around this time, the French physicist Dominique (Jean) Arago and Humphrey Davy also found that a cylindrical spire of copper wire through which an electric current was passed attracted iron filings as if they were a magnet, but that the filings fell away when the current ceased. Arago and Ampère also found that if a current was sent through a spiral of wire it magnetized steel needles wrapped in paper inside. Ampère, by 1820, was also well aware of the electromagnetic forces between parallel wires and their contrast with the electrostatic charges.

The concept that magnetism was related to electric currents was now quite obvious. The problem was how could it be utilised and controlled by man; there was much discussion and theorising in the scientific world of the day. Michael Faraday proved to be the man of the moment. His unique practical skills and fresh outlook, untrammelled by the need or expertise to prove his theories before tackling them, enabled him to eventually solve the problem of the link between electricity and magnetism with his visionary experiments.

Although not a mathematician himself, he relied on his own conception of lines of magnetic forces and electrical forces.

In 1821, we are told, Michael Faraday mounted a rigid copper wire able to turn about its point of suspension and hung it with the lower end in a bowl of liquid mercury; a vertical magnet was placed with one pole beneath the point of suspension. When a current was passed through the copper wire it swiftly spun round! Electromagnetic rotation resulted, for Michael Faraday had quite simply realised that the force surrounding the wire was circular! In 1824 he would be elected a very young Fellow of the Royal Society; a decision opposed by Sir Humphrey Davy who felt that Faraday had taken some of the glory of the chlorine development from him. But his former lab-boy and assistant would be promoted Laboratory Director of the Royal Institution the following year.

However, 1825 proved to be a very memorable year in the scientific calendar of events concerning electricity and magnetism. Jean Arago was not only the first Frenchman to receive the highly-esteemed Copley Medal from the Royal Society, but would also demonstrate that a rotating copper disk produced rotation in a magnetic needle suspended above it. Ampère, having brilliantly researched 'geometry shapes' on wires, then enunciated a system of mathematical laws; having found that currents have directions and different parts of a circuit may have different directions.

Also that year, the developments of magnetism by rotation led to the production of the first electromagnet in the form of a horseshoe by William Sturgeon, a native of Whittingham, Lancashire. His device is described as "a bent bar of soft iron about a foot long and half an inch in diameter (30 x 1.3 cms) coated with varnish, on which was wound a coil of 18 turns of bare copper wire". It is reported that when a current from a single wet battery cell was passed through the wire, the 7 oz bar (0.2 Kg) could support a 9 pounds iron mass (4 Kg), around twenty times its weight. During the next few years this method would be improved by Joseph Henry in the USA; his horseshoe magnet was covered with silk and the wire coil was copiously wound around the bar in the same direction. He subsequently made several versions; one when attached to a small battery could lift 75 pounds (34 Kg) and another up to 2086 pounds (946 Kg).

The hunt was on for the utilisation of these formidable powers contained within the combination of magnetism and electricity. Joseph Henry, during his experiments, had once noticed a spark in the coil when the current was broken, leading to the possibility of self-induction. He published in 1832. His work was unknown to Michael Faraday who made a similar experiment and was the first to publish. For by 1831 Michael Faraday, having continued his researches, proved without doubt what he had surmised for some time; the fact that magnetism could produce electricity. That an electric current produced a magnetic force and that a magnet acted on an electric current had already been shown. For ten days he carried out experiments demonstrating how electromagnetic induction could be achieved. It was another incredible step forward for mankind with electromagnetic interaction defined simply in terms of "magnetic lines of force, forming a field of force, which is distorted by the presence of a current-carrying conductor, or by another magnet."

A hundred years later, in 1931, the Institution of Electrical Engineers thought fit to hold centenary celebrations in London to mark his discoveries. His statue now stands outside their headquarters in Savoy Place, next to the former studio and offices of the BBC, not far from Waterloo Bridge. Resplendent in bronze and facing the Thames, a stone's throw from the Strand, the 'Father of Modern Electrical Science' modestly holds his now famous 'doughnut' induction coil for all to see. A man of unswerving integrity and deeply religious, Michael Faraday fervently believed the study of the physical world concerning the various forces of nature to be that of natural philosophy. He patented nothing.

The original coil he used in 1831 was made of soft iron with two different windings of insulated wire; the end of a copper wire was connected to a simple galvanometer. When the two ends of the other wire were permanently connected to a battery, there was no effect; but the galvanometer indicated a current if a circuit was made, or broken. A similar experiment was carried out using an iron cylinder and introducing and withdrawing magnets. Other modifications continued to show that a change of magnetic flow through a circuit produced a current in the circuit.

He also achieved the first dynamo by putting a rotating copper disc between the poles of a large electromagnet; resulting in an electric current being obtained from contacts with the axis and edge of the disc. His now immortal magnets and coils were quite simply induced to 'harness' electricity resulting in continuous motion; electrical power was generated. Gifted also with the ability to impart complex knowledge clearly and concisely, Michael Faraday, soon after becoming Laboratory Director in 1825, had instituted the Friday Evening Lectures for members of the Royal Institution; they still continued in a varied form.

Around this time, William Thomson, the later Lord Kelvin and eminent for his work on temperatures and much else, had been greatly impressed by the *Essay on the Application of Mathematical Analysis to the Theory of Electricity and Magnetism*, published in 1828. The author was George Green, of Sneinton, near Nottingham; a self-taught mathematician and son of a miller following in his father's trade. Expounding a two-dimensional method of solving mathematical problems, he published a few copies of his work at his own expense. He would write more and went to Cambridge University at the age of 40, but was dogged by ill-health and died eight years later. Lord Kelvin had the essay reprinted in 1846; five years after Green's death and three years after James Joule, the mostly self-taught Lancashire physicist, demonstrated the amount of work required to produce a unit of heat. Lord Kelvin would also apply his formidable scientific talents to the design of a special binnacle (the housing for the compass), by brilliantly using a series of magnets to compensate for the permanent and temporary magnetism of ships with steel hulls.

Meanwhile, the Scottish physicist, James Clerk Maxwell, enabled Michael Faraday's 'lines of force' to be treated mathematically by introducing the concept of the electromagnetic field. By then, during the 1830s, in Germany, Karl Gauss had made the first attempts to deduce the fundamental law of electromagnetic action in terms of an electric field; but the general idea that electrical effects are propagated in the form of waves was slow in developing. However, Maxwell observed the field radiating outwards from an oscillating electric charge did so at the speed of light; this led him to identify light as a form of electromagnetic radiation. He unified the theories of electricity, magnetism and light into a set of equations, also predicting Hertz's discovery of radio waves mathematically. *Maxwell's Equations* were published finally in 1873, a few years after the death of Michael Faraday.

It would not be until 1888 that Heinrich Hertz produced and detected radio waves. The unit of frequency is named after him. Hertz's further work on magnetic waves showed that their properties are in complete accordance with the waves of light and heat; establishing beyond doubt the electromagnetic nature of light. Independently from Maxwell, Ludwig Lorenz also visualized visible light as an electromagnetic phenomenon, rather than a stream of particles as suggested by Newton.

As we know from various verse forms learned at school, Isaac Newton 'separated light' by using a prism, resulting in the spectrum or 'rainbow'; otherwise the red, orange, yellow, green, blue, indigo and violet colours of the visible electromagnetic radiation of the sun. Michael Faraday attempted to find laws between light and magnetism using optical 'heavy glass'. He then discovered the rotation of the plane of the polarization of light in a magnetic field; an effect that occurs with quartz and known as the Faraday Effect. But by 1850 he was a very tired man and his last period of research was spent in trying to find a relationship between gravity and electricity. He died at his home in Surrey, in 1867, aged seventy-six.

Michael Faraday bequeathed to us not only the Faraday Constant, defined as "the quantity of electricity equivalent to 1 mole" whereby one mole is any substance containing $6.022.52 \times 10^{23}$ (quadrillion) each of atoms, molecules, ions, electrons etc, and the 'farad' as a unit of electrical capacitance, but also the legacy of his 'Christmas Courses of Lectures Adapted to a Juvenile Auditory'. Himself often an enthusiastic participant, they are still continued annually by invited scientists at the Royal Institution, beamed out on television and available on video to inform and delight worldwide.

CURRENTS AND CABLES

Save Our Souls! S O S . . . _ _ _ . . . *Latitude Longitude GMT*
(The Mayday (*m'aidez*) Morse Code signal of distress.)

The search for telegraphy by electrical means greatly intensified from the mid-18th century onwards. It was only a matter of time before further experimentation found that a 'voltaic current' could be used for transmitting signals. Some success was initially obtained by using electrolysis, observed by William Nicolson and Anthony Carlisle in 1800. This phenomenon, whereby the passage of an electric current caused the decomposition of liquids into their constituent elements, was utilised by early experimenters to design telegraph apparatus. The electrical decomposition of chemical compounds could be discerned at the end of conductors and their discharges interpreted as primitive signals.

In 1820, André Ampère, took up the suggestion of Pierre Laplace that the deflections of small magnets could be used to indicate letters of the alphabet. Telegraph instruments using needles soon came into being. The American physicist of Scottish descent, Joseph Henry, who had been apprenticed to a watchmaker when aged thirteen, was intrigued by the discovery that electromagnets could operate a considerable distance from a battery; around 1831 he constructed a successful electromagnetic signalling apparatus. In 1832 his fellow countryman, Samuel Morse, who was born in the same year as Michael Faraday, visited England and, we are told, became acquainted with his work. Returning home, Morse, a wealthy descendent of early English settlers and also a Yale graduate fascinated by chemistry and electricity, would also inspire a notable group of inventors and business men. In 1844, he produced a telegraph instrument and a few years later the first telegraph line began between Washington and

Baltimore. The famous code system of dots and dashes, devised to supersede the written and printed message, would take his name.

Meanwhile, in England, the one-time musical instrument maker and physicist, Charles Wheatstone, patented with his business partner William Fothergill Cooke, an early form of electric telegraph in 1837. This was developed primarily for signalling purposes by the newly built railway system. A system of electric telegraphy was used on the London and Birmingham line that year; it proved unsuitable to be widely practical.

However, a successful telegraph line soon ran along the Great Western Railway (GWR) line from Paddington Station in London to West Drayton, later extended to Slough; conveniently situated for use by Queen Victoria at Windsor Castle. By 1841 the railway reached Bristol. Put simply, a hand-operated key could be enabled to make or break a connection between a source of current. It was found that when the signalling apparatus was adapted with two deflecting needles, messages could be tapped along the connection by a code (connived from twenty letters of the alphabet) to the magnetic coil at the other end. The pulses of current passing to the distant end prompted the signal to be 'heard'. A model in 1845 would be Wheatstone and Cooke's most important invention. This used only a single needle. The Electric Telegraph Company was formed the same year.

Morse Code was first used commercially between England and France in 1851. The first submarine cables were composed of copper wires and covered with *gutta percha*; this black rubbery substance derived from sap was protected from the lusty appetites of sea creatures by a covering of brass plate plus a strong layer of steel wires covered in jute. Eventually, these cables could transmit Morse Code at a rate of 600 words per hour. In 1850, the first international telecommunications submarine cable had been laid between Dover on the south-east coast of England, across the English Channel, to Calais, on the north coast of France. The *Goliath*, a small paddle-driven steam tug, was charted for the work. The project was pioneered by John

Watkins Brett, son of a Bristol cabinet maker and now regarded as the 'father of submarine telegraphy'. Although working only briefly, the cable was successfully replaced the following year. John Brett and his brother Jacob would register companies that revolutionised the commercial systems of the world, linking Britain not only with France but also eventually to Ireland, Nova Scotia, India and the colonies.

In 1858, the 3,500 ton battleship *HMS Agamemnon* and the US steam frigate *Niagara* met in mid-Atlantic; they then set off in opposite directions to lay the first transatlantic cable. This linked Ireland and the USA successfully for a brief period until the insulation began to fail. This project was masterminded and financed from the USA by the paper merchant and tycoon Cyrus West Field, founder of the New York, Newfoundland and London Telegraph Company and friend of Lord Kelvin. Field was also helped during his initial pioneering with essential information supplied by Matthew Fontaine Maury, a former midshipman who, after being disabled in an accident, built up the US Naval Observatory and Hydrographic Office. He would become Professor of Meteorology at the Virginia Military Institute and has been referred to as the 'father of oceanography'; the science of the sea.

The Atlantic Telegraph Company was soon formed in Great Britain with the help of Cyrus Field. In 1865, Captain James Anderson was chosen by the Cunard Company to command Isambard Kingdom Brunel's *Great Eastern*; chartered by the Atlantic Telegraph Company to lay their new cable. On 23 July 1865, the *Great Eastern* sailed from Valentia Island off Kerry in SW Ireland and laid 1186 nautical miles (2196 Km) of cable until it broke. Undeterred, the following year the *Great Eastern* retrieved the end of the cable, successfully spliced it and completed the transatlantic linkage to the somewhat appropriately named Heart's Content in Newfoundland on 8 September 1866.

Fittingly, there was a newspaper published on board, the *Great Eastern Telegraph 1866*. Copies contain accounts of the messages sent between Queen Victoria and the US President, as well as other news received at sea including Greenwich Mean Time. Honours were bestowed on Cyrus Field and Captain Anderson received a knighthood. He was assisted throughout by Chief Officer Robert Halpin; an expert navigator who would become the *Great Eastern*'s longest serving commander.

The Glasgow cotton magnate, John Pender, was also an investor in the Atlantic Telegraphy Company; inspired by the success of the submarine cable he pioneered a network. As chairman of the Telegraph and Maintenance Company, his companies would own one third of the world's submarine cable and operate ten cable ships. Two global businesses would result; Cable and Wireless and Global Marine Systems Ltd.

The development of the cable ships and laying the submarine cables was fraught with hazards and dangers. In 1885 the cable ship *Magneta* left England for Singapore and was never heard of again. Ship-to-shore radio communications were not introduced until the early 1900s, some three decades after ships had begun to be specifically designed for cable laying and maintenance operations. The design of these cable ships would remain very much the same for nearly a century.

Guglielmo Marconi would open the first wireless telegraph service across the Atlantic in 1907. By the 1920s international telegraph messages were being sent manually by submarine cable and using code keys; they were translated manually at the receiving end. Some of the technical equipment used in the early days can now be seen at the Museum of Submarine Telegraphy based in Porthcurno at the southernmost tip of Cornwall.

A small hut near Gwennap Head, on a secluded slightly-sloping beach free of fishing vessels, was used as the starting point for the underwater cables to send their 'instant' messages. Two lines went out to Gibraltar, one for transmitting and the other for receiving. Initially, one message only could be sent at a time. Submarine telephony would also become possible with short cables in shallow water. The first 'repeater' installation in a submarine telephone cable was achieved in

1943 between Anglesey in Wales and the Isle of Man. This was made possible by the invention of polyethylene and the development of the 'co-axial' cables system which incorporated 'repeaters' or amplifiers; inserted in the circuit at intervals and boosting the strength and fidelity of the signals, thus making possible transmission over long distances.

The first international co-axial cables linked England and Holland in 1947. By 1956 they had advanced to carry a signal more than 33,000 miles (53,000 Km) and capable of relaying it five times in less than one minute; a total of half a million nautical miles of cable encircled the globe beneath the ocean waves. Although by the mid-1950s there were six and a half million telephone users in the UK and fifty million in the USA, telephony across the Atlantic Ocean was neither frequent nor economic; in 1927 the first radio-telephone link cost around £15 for three minutes. This was remedied in August 1956 with the installation of the first two transoceanic submarine telephone cables; one reaching across the Atlantic from Newfoundland to Oban.

With the installation of the transatlantic co-axial cable system, the TAT-1, voices were transmitted under the ocean, ninety years and eighteen days after the first successful transatlantic submarine cable was laid in 1866. The first Pacific co-axial cable was introduced in 1963, sixty years after a submarine telegraph cable was laid under the ocean from New Zealand to Canada. Digital technology would make possible the first fibre optic submarine telephone communication system. These modern cables have a minimum core of two one-way glass fibres; each thinner than a human hair, coated in acrylic and capable of transmitting light pulses generated by lasers (Light Amplification by Stimulated Emission of Radiation) carrying millions of simultaneous telephone calls or data transactions. Initially installed in 1986 from Belgium to the UK, by 1998 the first transatlantic fibre optic system was in operation, the TAT-8.

The year 2000 saw the fibre optics cable system transmitting millions of simultaneous telephone calls as 205,000 miles (330,000

Km) of fibre optic cables encircled the world; a single fibre in a submarine telecommunications cable can carry 15 million voicing circuits. Digital TV and data traffic also now surge along cables laid four miles (6 Km) under the oceans. Advanced computer technology and satellite communications have greatly aided the accuracy of cable-laying operations. By 1995 the launch of the 3 CS Cable Innovator had introduced facilities to enable the laying and recovering of cables in the stern of the ship, thus allowing work to continue in bad weather unless conditions become grossly unsuitable.

There are many types of machine used on the seabed to aid the installation and maintenance of submarine cable; some machines cut into the rocks to complete the security of the cable and others recover cable for repair. More than 8000 Km of cable can now be accommodated on a single trip, equivalent to 4,750 nautical miles; a transatlantic system may take up to two weeks to load. The submarine cable telecommunications industry has provided one of the greatest economic and social changes the world has ever seen. From the initial twelve hours of 'instant' telegraphy to reach Darwin in Northern Australia, where to the south the town of Alice Springs would be named after the wife of the superintendent of telegraphs, Sir Charles Todd, the world of science would know no bounds as the dots and dashes of universal communication opened up frontiers by technological feats. These took a century and a half to achieve, and paved the way for the dot.com revolution of today.

ISAAC NEWTON AND ALBERT EINSTEIN REASON AND RELATIVITY IN THE HEAVENS OF WILLIAM HERSCHEL AND EDWIN HUBBLE

> *"Nature and Nature's Laws lay hid in Night:*
> *God said, 'Let Newton be! and All was Light."*

Penned by the poet and satirist Alexander Pope as an epitaph to Sir Isaac Newton, only to be later double-parodied by Sir John Collings Squire:

> *"It did not last: the Devil howling 'Ho!*
> *Let Einstein be!' restored the status quo."*

Isaac Newton, on returning to Cambridge University when it reopened in 1668 after an outbreak of plague, was elected Professor of Mathematics and Physical Science. He was aged twenty-six and had spent his eighteen months of enforced exile 'thinking at home' at the family farm in Lincolnshire at Woolsthorpe-by-Colsterworth, some 8 miles (12km) from Grantham where his statue now stands in front of the civic buildings facing the shopping centre named in his honour. As we know, his time was not wasted for Isaac Newton's contemplations would lead to the discoveries of calculus, spectrum analysis and the laws of gravity; the foundation of modern physics. His *Principia Mathematica* propounding the laws of 'celestial mechanics', otherwise what he considered to be going on around and above us was, to a great extent, very accurate.

Put very simply, his account of the construction of the universe has gone down in history for suggesting:

a) that light was composed of units or particles emitted from a luminous source, the sun, and travelling in a vacuum, otherwise space.

b) that calculus, a particular method of calculation, was based on the concept of infinitely small changes in continuously varying particles.

c) that the velocity of a moving body was defined as the rate of change of its position at any instant.

Isaac Newton would reject the elementary 'wave theory' of light. He could not then know that waves of light might be exceedingly small; preferring the theory that light was a 'corpuscular' phenomenon composed of minute bodies. That sunlight or 'white light' is not only sensitive to the human eye but is, in fact, visible electromagnetic radiation was demonstrated by James Clerk Maxwell towards the end of the 19th century. Neither is it 'white', for the daylight we experience is a mixture of all colours of the spectrum; with a range of intensity from 400 nanometers in extreme violet to 770 nanometers in the extreme red ('nano' being defined as a thousandth million). In 1881 the famous experiment was carried out in America by Albert Michelson and Edward Morley to ascertain the speed of light. They used a specially designed instrument, the interferometer; the name is derived from the scientific term for waves of light striking against each other, the 'interference'. Light would be calculated to travel at 670 million miles per hour (1078 million Km).

In 1905, Albert Einstein, also aged twenty-six and with a PhD in science from the University of Zurich in Switzerland, was working in a low-grade job assessing applications in the Patent Office in Berne due to financial necessity, unable to find an academic position. This interim humble post allowed him, however, the time to puzzle that 'light speed' was the only absolute constant, otherwise the highest attainable speed in the universe at 186,000 miles per second (299,000 Km). He was much influenced by the 'quantum theory' formulated by the Berlin University physicist Max Planck a few years earlier in 1900 that "electromagnetic radiation (EMR) is emitted in 'packets' or 'quantities' rather than a steady stream and a photon is a quantity of EMR."

Being greatly intrigued that the smallest quantities of energy in which light is emitted, the photons, were existent alongside the wave theory, led Albert Einstein to formulate 'relativity' and 'time-space' as another dimension. The earlier scientific observations had concluded that light always travels at the same uniform speed, no matter the speed of its source. It was, therefore, the absolute constant in the universe. Thus, in 1905 he published his now famous papers on the molecular construction of matter, the quantum theory of radiation, the photoelectric effect in terms of photons and the relativity of mass to energy. His unique exposition on the *Theory of Relativity*, or making sense of the relationship between time and space, took five weeks of exhausting work in order to transmute his ideas into a mathematic progression. It would appear as a paper entitled *On the Electrodynamics of Motion*.

Thus the pacifist Albert Einstein proved theoretically with his equation $E=mc^2$ (E=energy, m=mass and c=the speed of light) that the energy contained in a substance equalled its mass multiplied by the speed of light. It would be discovered that the 'substance' could be a highly radioactive naturally-occurring metallic element, such as uranium with 92 protons and 146 neutrons contained in the nucleus of one atom. Many heavy atoms and isotopes heavier than lead were found to be radioactive. The conversion of this energy for destructive purposes would be phenomenol.

A new terminology came into our language and from our schooldays we are familiar with the names and facts of basic science; that the atoms in an element are concentrated in the nucleus which consists of positively-charged 'protons' and neutrally-charged 'neutrons'. The electrons exist around a nucleus in 'shells' of particular energy levels. The chemical behaviour of an atom is largely determined by the number of electrons in the outermost shell. The proton is 1836 times heavier than an electron. 'Particle physics' came into being with the discovery of the electron in 1897, the proton in 1911 and the neutron in 1932.

However, in 1919, Albert Einstein was busy deducing that space and time cannot exist alone, but only in the presence of matter and without the mass of the universe there could be no gravity. In fact, mass, time, space and gravitation are interdependent on each other;

that there is no such thing as 'empty space'. For if the speed of light never changes, the distance travelled by it when divided by the time taken gives the 'time-rate', hence 'relativity'. Gravity, he would conclude, was curved space. Thus, his revolutionary theory predicted that even light was subject to the effects of gravity, for if space and time are regarded as 'physical entities curved by the gravitational fields of massive objects such as stars and galaxies', this meant that light from distant stars could be 'bent' by a large body of mass, such as the sun; consequently the light would reach the Earth in a slightly curved path.

In May 1919, Einstein's theory was quickly confirmed when Britain mounted an expedition to a small island, Principe, off equatorial West Africa to observe a solar eclipse; led by Arthur Eddington, Professor of Astronomy at Cambridge University and previously, from 1906-1913, Chief Assistant at the Royal Observatory Greenwich. An expert on the structure of stars, he had come to the conclusion that the energy emitted as light and heat from the surface of a star was also transmitted internally in the form of radiation; also, that the mass and luminosity were related. He was deeply interested in Einstein's general theory of relativity and data and photographs obtained of the total eclipse on Principe, now in archives, proved that the positions of the stars seen just beyond the eclipsed solar disc were 'slightly displaced from the centre of the disc'. As Albert Einstein had predicted theoretically, light from distant stars was indeed 'bent' by the gravity of the sun. He would be awarded the Nobel Prize for Physics in 1921.

Just two centuries after Newton's death, a large machine for 'accelerating' beams of charged particles by electric fields, either in a straight line or circle controlled by magnetic fields, was developed in 1932 by Yorkshireman John Cockroft and Irishman Ernest Walton at the Cavendish Laboratory in Cambridge. Their linear accelerator in which particles moved at near the speed of light resulted in the splitting of the atom; their work was officially described as having 'successfully disintegrated the nuclei of lithium and other light elements by protons entirely artificially generated by high energy potentials'.

An 'atomic theory' of the universe had been put forward around 400 BC by Democritius, much influenced by his mentor, Leucippus. Developing his materialistic view of nature, he would write also of cosmology, biology, perception and music. But it would be another two thousand years before the English chemist John Dalton researched 'gases' and came up with his laws of 'partial pressures' and 'multiple proportions', leading around 1803 to his theory that all matter is composed of particles; but he did not distinguish between atoms and molecules.

Another two centuries would find New Zealander Ernest Rutherford, researching at the Cavendish Laboratory, discovering that alpha, beta and gamma rays were constituents of radioactivity. With his colleague, Hans Geiger, he discovered that the alpha rays were composed of helium atoms. These had very positive charges; when bombarded onto gold foil each atom appeared to have a very heavily charged core, the 'nucleus'.

Man's search for knowledge would lead to the energy of nuclear fission. When the heavy atomic nucleus of uranium is split into two or more parts, then the total mass of the parts is less than the mass of the original nucleus. The difference in mass, equivalent to the binding energy of the nucleus, is converted into kinetic energy; the increased velocity that results in explosion. Nuclear fusion occurs when two light nuclei combine to form a stable nucleus, such as helium. When a resulting nucleus is lighter than the sum of the component nuclei, again kinetic energy is released. A hydrogen atom has only one single proton as its nucleus. Each nucleus of an atom of an element contains the same number of protons, but not always the same number of neutrons. Those elements with a different number of neutrons in the nucleus of their atoms are known as isotopes. They have the same chemical but different physical properties. The 'mass number' of an element is the value of both protons and neutrons.

The nuclear energies of fission and fusion both demonstrate

Einstein's theory, $E = mc^2$. Atomic research took off; the Danish physicist Niels Bohr would expound on the orbiting electron atomic theory. In the USA Robert Millikan would measure the charge on the electron; Henry Taube would study the loss or gain of electrons by atoms during chemical reactions. There was much research by many scientists in various countries. In 1939 the implications of the nuclear fission of uranium were known by the German physicist Otto Hahn; he was unwilling to publish. Niels Bohr, in Copenhagen, would also find out; when visiting America, he would tell Einstein who would also learn of the danger of Germany developing an atomic bomb from other refugee scientists. Einstein felt obliged to write and warn President Roosevelt. The USA then initiated the Manhattan Project; atomic warfare became a reality. Japan would arrange for the supply of the necessary radioactive isotopes from Germany. A submarine transporting some of these materials en route in 1945 was obliged to surrender to the USA as peace was declared in Europe.

The first atomic explosion in 1945 at Hiroshima released heat, light and radiation to a power of 20,000 tons of TNT. The first hydrogen bomb was detonated by America at Eniwetok Atoll in 1952 with an estimated power of millions of tons of TNT; composed of an atom bomb creating the necessary temperature to ignite a surrounding layer of hydrogenous material. Subsequently made and tested by several other major powers, the hydrogen bomb has never been used in war. A simple paraphrase of a well-known nursery rhyme, reputedly once found written on the wall of a college physics laboratory, perhaps sums up very eloquently and succinctly the advent of the atomic age:

A ring, a ring of protons,
A pocket full of neutrons,
A fission,
A fusion,
We all fall down.

Albert Einstein took no part in the manufacture of the atomic weapons that resulted from his theory of relativity. With the end of WWII he became actively involved with nuclear disarmament. In the year Einstein died, Niels Bohr organised the Atoms for Peace Conference. The Campaign for Nuclear Disarmament (CND) in Britain began three years later, in 1958. Apart from a revival in the 1980s the lessening of East-West tensions contributed to its decline. The Greenpeace Movement was begun in 1971 and still campaigns as an international environmental pressure group; particularly in relation to the adverse effects of nuclear power and nuclear waste used commercially.

Britain's first nuclear reactor had been installed at the Atomic Energy Research Establishment at Harwell in 1946; the previous year Sir John Cockroft had been appointed Director. Most commercial reactors were initially based on the fusion principle and therefore thermal; but subsequently gradually replaced by the 'fast' or 'breeder' reactors which, by a process of 'escaping' neutrons into a 'blanket' of natural uranium are fifty times more economical in their usage.

The world's first nuclear power station opened at Calder Hall in Cumbria during 1956; using uranium 239 and its by-product plutonium, produced in large quantities in nuclear reactors by beta-decay, the resultant fission was harnessed to produce heat at a controlled rate for powering turbines. A very small amount of nuclear fuel provides a very large amount of energy; an approximate comparison being that of 700 billion joules per Kg of nuclear fuel compared to 400 million joules per Kg of coal. This is of particular significance for submarine power. Despite reservations, by 1991 more than a third of electricity supply in Europe was provided by nuclear energy; considered essential because of the diminishing supplies of fossil fuel.

We know now that since the 1960s more that two hundred elementary particles have been identified and two classes of these, the 'leptons' and 'quarks' have emerged; the latter having very fractional electronic charges, possibly the smallest particle in the universe, the fundamental constituent of all matter and possibly providing evidence for the Big Bang Theory. It has been observed that if that fundamental constituent of all matter, the atom, so-named from the Greek *atomos* for indivisible, be considered as having the area of a large cathedral, then its nucleus in the centre would be the size of a flea.

The forces of gravity and electromagnetism are now known to be complemented by 'strong' and 'weak' interactions but the activity of the mysterious energies contained within the nucleus by the electrons, neutrons and protons is, however, a very complex subject and perhaps can be visualised in the words sometime whimsically penned:

> *Great fleas have little fleas upon their backs to bite them,*
> *And little fleas have lesser fleas and so on ad infinitum.*
> *And the great fleas, themselves in turn,*
> *Have greater fleas to go on,*
> *Whilst those again have greater still,*
> *And greater still and so on.*

The development of atomic science would inevitably lead to the 'space race' and the search for the rocket-engine. In 1903 a paper had been published in Russia on the use of rockets in space travel; a few years later crude TV pictures would also be developed in Russia using inventions from German and England; the Nipkow Disc and Crooke's Cathode-Ray Tube.

In 1929, Edwin Hubble, one-time Rhodes Scholar at Oxford, later on the astronomy staff of the Carnegie Institution of Washington's Mount Wilson Observatory with its 100-inch telescope (250 cm), would record the fascinatingly-named 'Hubble's Law of the Red Shifts'. This described the speed of nebulae increasing in a linear manner with distance. Put simply, galaxies beyond our own galaxy were running away from us, thus confirming an expanding universe. Hubble's Constant or H_0 denotes the rate at which the velocity of expansion of the universe changes with distance, otherwise the relationship between the running-away speed of the galaxy and that of the distance run.

Post WWII the humble heat-producing thermionic valve (or vacuum tube) with its prolific flow of electrons, those units of negative electricity normally, but not always, rotating at mysterious speeds about the positive nucleus of every atom, would eventually be developed into 'solid-state' electronic appliances; without moving parts and minute enough to be contained in a small spacecraft. Thus, 1949 would herald in the transistor and later the multi-transistor circuits in the form of silicon chips, compact and low in energy consumption; making possible the communication marvels of the space age using computers reckoning electronically with memory and time.

In 1969 the first man walked on the moon. By end of the next decade, the spacecraft *Pioneer* and *Voyager* reached the planets Venus and Jupiter, travelling at 1/26,000 the speed of light; the first personal computer was available for home use and would rapidly decline in price. In the 1990s and nearly four centuries after the death of Elizabeth I, we could see the unbelievable mission by NASA astronauts to repair – in space – the world's first Hubble Space Telescope.

After launching it had developed a flaw in its 2.3 metre-wide mirror (7.5 ft) comprising one ton of glass; caused by a flake of paint the size of 1/50 of a strand of human hair! Five gruelling space walks were required to put in a new camera, achieved with incredible precision. Now successfully researching at 17,000 mph (27,360 kph) the thousands of galaxies 300 miles (483 Km) above us, some estimated to be twelve billion years old, the spellbinding photographs taken by Hubble 1 can be seen by us at home; a successor is planned with an 8-metre diameter mirror (26 ft). For when reproduced on TV, the photographs present a magical and unimaginably majestic kaleidoscope of the universe surrounding Earth with its great magnetic iron core. William Herschel and many others would be more than a little astonished, but perhaps not totally unsurprised, especially Isaac Newton whose 'thinking at home' was so momentous for mankind, but also extremely reassuring that it was not the burden of individual sins that kept feet on the ground, just an interactive process whereby a body is attracted to the centre of the earth or other planets by the forces occasioned by the existence of mass anywhere in the universe. The Latin word 'gravitas' meaning 'weight' summed up the situation very succinctly.

Courtesy of the National Trust we can now visit Isaac Newton's home and see the room at Woolsthorpe Manor where he was born and, just along the landing, the study overlooking the apple orchard. A full-scale replica of his small but famous telescope (the original is at the Royal Society) is there with other possessions.

Outside, we can walk through the farmyard where hens, ponies and hay are still much in evidence to the converted barn which now serves as a very stimulating Science Centre.

TV TIMES – MONITORS AND COMPUTERS WITH CHIPS

"To look at you, one would not think you held so many secrets, but I know better..."

Winston Churchill addressing personnel at Bletchley Park, the highly-secret 'Station X', during WWII.

A few years after Edwin Hubble's discovery in 1929, Cambridge University conferred a Professorship in Mathematics on the 23-year-old Alan Turing; then working on a paper concerning a hypothetical 'thinking machine'. Later, when based at the WWII secret coding station at Bletchley Park in Buckinghamshire, he turned his formidable talent to mechanising 'number functions'. His genius pioneered electrically-operated 'intelligent thinking machines', the Turing Bombes, resulting in the deciphering of the German Enigma code by automation.

Alan Turing and the Bletchley Park team would go on to break the even more sophisticated code of the German Lorenz machine; achieved by the construction of the world's first electronic-programmable computer, Colossus. Using initially 2,500 radio valves obtained from the GPO and upgraded by D-Day, its construction would be unknown of after the war; Bletchley Park kept its secrets for many years. Volunteers have recently rebuilt a full-scale model; now on view for all to see. Towards the end of WWII, in America, John Von Neumann published a paper mathematically formulating a machine based on a central control unit; the processor, with a random access read/write memory. Thus, by 1945 the theoretical groundwork was complete.

Meanwhile, the possibility of television available universally was getting off the ground. The cathode-ray tube had been invented by William Crookes in the UK in 1878. His discovery that cathode rays consist of charged particles led to the development of the vacuum tube being utilised as a site for the conversion of the electrical signals, emitted by the charged particles, to form black and white visible images on a fluorescent screen. The British electrical engineer, John Logie Baird, experimented and developed the transmission of these images first as outlines of shapes, then features and eventually moving objects during the early 1920s. By 1928 he had produced colour television pictures. Although his 240-line system was not adopted by the BBC, nevertheless his work laid the foundations for the television of today. He also pioneered radar and fibre optics. The television monitor screen appeared. By 1948, Alan Turing was at Manchester University with Professors Williams and Kilburn and experimenting with cathode-ray tubes for memory storage. They built a small 'computer' that executed a programme. This was linked up to a monitor screen. By 1951, after joining forces with a local electronics firm, the Ferranti Mark 1 was marketed. During the same year the USA came out with Univac 1; the first computer to use magnetic tape.

Meanwhile, in Cambridge, Professor Wilkes produced the Electronic Delay Storage Automatic Calculator (EDSAC), which the Manchester team upgraded with the world's first-ever 'library' of programmes. Subsequent collaboration with catering firm, Joe Lyons, successfully pioneered the use of computers for business data processing. Radio valves would be replaced by 'transistors' using the thermionic (or vacuum) valves which allowed a much greater flow of electrons to provide the energy; thus amplifying and controlling electric currents and miniaturising the components required. The Manchester ATLAS computer, introduced in 1963, was then considered the fastest in the world.

And so on, until today when we have the marvel of the 'chip' derived from crystals of the element silicon; the simple sand of beach and desert and essential constituent of the personal computer. Initially, a code number was given to a silicon chip, the Central Processing Unit (CPU) which did the 'thinking' of the first personal computers. These were the 8086-based computers, which then astonishingly handled incoming data at a rate of 8 bits (equivalent to one byte) at a time.

The byte would be 'read' as a single instruction and then 'sent' to perform essential tasks such as making a programme proceed to the next instruction, placing a letter or figure on the screen or sending signals to the printer. Now we deal in gigabytes (Gb) equal to one million bytes per second. A clock measured the actual computing speed of a CPU by units measured in megahertz. Very soon the data could be handled at 16 bits a time; twice the speed and producing the 80826, until gigahertz (GHz) came into common usage. The transmission of data would be known by the Baud Rate, approximately the equivalent of bits per second.

The manufacturers of the chips, Intel, decided to dispense with numbers and upgrade to names. The supremo was the Pentium, designed for heavy commercial, or highly specialized, computing; with a silicon chip approximately only one square cm in size, but containing several million transistors. Electronic cameras, known as scanners, would provide the storing of images in various graphical formats or 'standards'. By means of the Optical Character Recognition (OCR) examining the electronic snapshot taken by the camera, each letter of a printed page could be converted to text. The highly competitive marketing of hardware and software needed for the booting, or starting, a computer with the hard or floppy disks containing their operating systems, the DOS, also arrived. The rest, as they say, is history.

JOHN 'LONGITUDE' HARRISON
– LIFE AT BARROW UPON HUMBER

When Henry Harrison moved around 1697 to Barrow upon Humber, probably from the estate of Nostell Priory near Wakefield in Yorkshire, he could not have foreseen that his new village, then with around 700 inhabitants, would one day be internationally associated with the monumental achievement in adulthood of his four year old son; and of which he, himself, would lay the foundations. The young John would have two brothers and sisters. From their father the boys learned joinery and, it seems, the mending of timepieces.

John and James plied at their father's trade in a workshop to the rear of the Royal Oak tavern, still very much in existence today. Helped initially by his brother, John Harrison completed his first pendulum clock in 1713, made almost entirely from wood. Others followed in 1715 and 1717. He married in 1718 for the first time. In 1720 came the commission for a tower clock from Sir Charles Pelham at his new stables at Brocklesby Park, Habrough, just 12 miles south of Barrow on Humber.

The gently methodical and soothing rhythm of this now much-mellowed clock still keeping regular time can also be enjoyed today, courtesy of another Charles Pelham, the 8th Earl of Yarborough who succeeded in 1991. Another craftsman joiner, Mr Harry Johnson, resident on the estate for over four decades, will happily explain the workings and indicate the inscription by John Harrison of his name and village on the clock; it is just visible today with a magnifier. Visitors from far and wide are by no means infrequent.

John Harrison compiled a table enabling him to rectify the difference between solar time as shown by the sundial and mean time, whereby each day is regulated to be of 24 hours duration throughout the year. It is recorded that he called this conversion table *A table of the sun rising and setting in the latitude of Barrow upon Humber 53 degree 18 minutes*. Two further long case clocks were built by the brothers from 1725-27, incorporated John's pioneering gridiron pendulum and grasshopper escapement. They kept near perfect time.

Personal tragedy struck in 1726 when John Harrison's young wife died. He was not a widower for long and around this period moved his family into the cottage at 122 Barton Lane, not far from the Royal Oak tavern where it is believed he continued to keep his workshop adjacent to the rear yard. His father died in 1728; Henry Harrison's will records 'Chattels and Credits' for a total of £151 15sh 5d.

In 1732 James made the sundial which can be seen today, on request, in the parish church of Holy Trinity in Barrow. Both brothers were very musical. John was Choirmaster at Holy Trinity and retuned the bells at Barrow Church and possibly he was involved in a similar mission at a church in Hull. He is certainly known to have carried out work on the bell frame in the church at Thornton Curtis a few miles away from Barrow; documentation from the church accounts of the period verifies this.

The nearby Thornton Abbey with its impressive ruined gatehouse was founded in 1139 as a house for Augustinian canons; some five centuries after a church is known to have existed in Barrow. Around 677 AD St Chad, Bishop of Mercia and Lindisfarne, is recorded as being given 50 hides of land to build a monastery by King Wulfstan. Evidence of this building has been found and is commemorated in Barrow at St Martin's Close, just around the corner from John Harrison Close and north-east of the present church of Holy Trinity. It is noted by the present churchwarden, John P W Cherry, in his publication 'A Short Guide', that extracts from the excavations on the site can be seen at Baysgarth Museum at Barton upon Humber, three miles west of Barrow.

It is considered that the church of St Chad was probably destroyed by invading Danes in 871 AD and that the present building of Holy

Trinity began around 1000 AD. Apart from its more famous associations, the church is well worth a visit in its own right. The perpendicular tower, clearly visible when walking up the High Street from the market place where the bus stops outside the Royal Oak by the present Post Office, now glories in eight bells; also very popular from far and wide with visiting campanologists. Originally there were six bells, dated 1636, 1638, 1649 and 1674; these would have been the ones known and used by John Harrison. He might be pleased to know that some three centuries later, in 1952, the bells were recast and another two added.

John Harrison moved permanently to London with his family in 1736; he was then forty-five. James Harrison eventually become a bell-founder and was for a time a miller in another village. He died in 1766 and John made over the property at 122 Barton Lane to James' son, also of the same name. The cottage has been described as "a typical single storey with three main ground floor rooms and attic 'chambers' lit by dormer windows". Archives show that it remained occupied by the Harrison family until 1789. The last recorded occupant by 1843 was that of the Reverend Nelson Graburn and the establishment is described as 'cottage, croft & maltkin'.

It would seem that the site would contain one of Barrow's breweries and then facilities for a seed merchant. In 2002 a parishioner of Barrow, also churchwarden, could verify that the dwelling was very habitable, and certainly lived in, until its very untoward demolition in 1968 to make way for a larger entrance to the seed merchants and then for the new 'Millfields' housing estate in the 1990's..

Possibly due to the fact that there are no known family archives of John Harrison's descendents in the area, interest in his early years where he pioneered his first and not wholly unsuccessful accurate sea-going clock H1, has remained low profile.

However, a few dedicated individuals have devoted their energies to keeping his achievements published. Apart from Lt. Commander Rupert T Gould in 1935 with his article in *The Mariner's Mirror*,

Colonel H Quill's studies with the *Notes and Records of the Royal Society* in 1963, the *Antiquarian Horological Society* in 1976 and *The Man Who Found Longitude* around the same time were followed in 1993 with publications by Dr Jonathan Betts, Curator of Horology at the National Maritime Museum and in 1995 with the Lincolnshire County Council's *From A Peal of Bells: John Harrison 1693-1776* by A King.

The bicentenary of his death in 1976, was celebrated by a pageant in the streets of Barrow. In 1981 the village school would be named after him. The tercentenary of his birth, in 1993, would bring major exhibitions at Greenwich and Lincoln. Today, local interest remains very much alive. A number of inhabitants collaborated with the publication in 1999 of *John Harrison's Village*, in conjunction with the research of the Workers' Education Association (WEA) during classes held in Barrow during 1994-98. A project that would no doubt have delighted John Harrison, often considered a self-taught man himself.

However, knowledge must have been obtainable and possibly more significantly communicated than perhaps realised. Records tend to be sparse. Possibly some avenues were too commonplace to mention; 'word of mouth' providing veritable trade routes of knowledge for those who cared to listen and learn. Henry Harrison had been parish clerk for several decades and no doubt he was used to visiting clergy, maybe his family talking to and entertaining them. For we do know that in 1712, when John Harrison was nineteen a visiting cleric lent him a copy of some lectures on mechanics by one Nicholas Saunderson. He copied out the whole book and we are told that it remained a life-long treasured possession, annotated with 'copious notes'.

An unidentified short term resident of Barrow would pithily record in verse and with obvious intimacy of the personal habits of many of the inhabitants, shrewd observations of life in the village around 1878/9. This clandestine activity came only to the light of day by the discovery around 1922 of a document in a building which had been used as a post-office at that time.

Penned on official government embossed paper, the document has been declared authentic for the names of many of the people mentioned could be traced from the commercial registers of that era in the archives, including one James Metham whose shop had been used for post-office services. A clue to the possible authorship, apart from the connection with the post-office could perhaps be that the clergymen of the parish are not much commented on; whether intentional or by default is open to conjecture.

By then it was just over a century after John Harrison's death. Although the population had by then trebled, perhaps a wry chuckle might have been heard emanating from his family tomb at St John's Church in Hampstead at the descriptions and goings-on in the village he knew so well, far away in North Lincolnshire. The Barrow upon Humber WEA classes thought fit to reproduce it in their publication of *John Harrison's Village*. With their permission it is included here:–

A Descriptive Account of a few Barrow People etc by 'One who has resided there'

Anon. 1878-9. (Abridged).

Mr Drake keeps a trap
  Mr Batson mends the tap
Mr Stainton deals in wood
  Mr Maw is very good
Mr Walker was very near
  Old John Glover likes his beer
Joseph Hill is very thin
  Mr Pearson likes gin
Metham keeps a grocer's shop
  "General" Brown sells very good pop
Jeremy Brown deals in locks
  Mr Gray mends watches and clocks
Mr Edwards makes good breeches
  Mr Heall takes neat stitches
Mr Tinning's a jolly old fellow
  Old Sparks Sergeants bulls do bellow
Mr Gelder mends the plough
  Old Miss Jones keeps a cow
Mr Uppleby is the squire
  Mr Stainton mends his fire
John Bilton has a nag that canters
  "Billy Hamilton's" at the head of the "ranters"
It was a grand sight last Barrow fair
  To see "Joe Fiddle" & Clara the loving pair
Young Miss Rawlin likes her cat
  Maria Tomlinson is very fat
Samuel Dee bothered his life
  With thrashing and calling his poor wife
One night when drunk and the wind did blow
  Tommy Robinson jumped up & began to crow

Mr Johnson is the tinner
>> Hiram Hoodlass is a sinner
Bryan Cooper makes saddles and whips
>> But Mr Dannatt trades with his ships
The three oldest persons in this our town
>> One Peggy Jump & his wife & old "Hezzy" Brown
Mr Smith in Barrow, makes your beer
>> And he and his wife are very dear
Of children he has just got six
>> Susannah, Ada & Minnie the 'vix'
There's Sarah Ann and Clara the nob
>> But the crown of the lot is their brother "BOB"
We've got gas in Barrow but that you all Know
>> But the maker of it's a man name Snow
John Simonds keeps the Royal Oak
>> Where drunkards go to drink and smoke
Mr Howson deals in fish
>> Which consists of some herrings stuck on a dish
He's got cods and lings which are cut in nice steaks
>> Mussles, cockles, plaice, sprats & a few old hakes
On Saturday night about eight o'clock
>> People come to this shop in a regular flock
They kick a row and bellow and roar
>> And folks wish the old fish shop would open no more
I'll now say a little about Marriott the bobby
>> When dressed up so fine he thinks himself nobby
When in his bright buttons and fine coat of blue
>> He looks like a card-board stuck together with glue
Whene'er there's a row he's out of his place
>> But when the row's o'er he comes at neck breaking pace
John Stainton's the sexton as well as the clerk
>> He does his work well and is fond of a lark

But at church on a Sunday, the boys are in fears
        For he often goes to them and clatters their ears
Mr Metham got married some time ago
        Miss Elizabeth Dinsdale was his beaux
He soon got tired of single life
        And so he took a second wife
On the 23rd of last March he jumped for joy
        Because his wife delivered him a fine boy
On a night ('tis said) he nurses it gently
        But at last he's come up with his good friend Bentley
Poor Alfred Boyle has gone at last
        And with him much of the fun that's past
At Barrow Schools he had a long stay
        And some felt sorry at his going away
But the reason he went 'tis hard to tell
        but where'ver he goes I hope he'll do well
Robert Newham the Red Lion keeps
        And under his roof "Starchy Clayton" sleeps
Mr Drake has got a new buss
        And Mr Gooseman wears a truss
Mr Austin now resides in this town
        In Slasher Cooper's house of renown
James Barrick is a basket maker
        But in Barrow we haven't a baker
Young James has come to mend clocks & watches
        And Derry Hutton kills pigs on cratches
Abraham Allison is a miller
        Edward Barratt good beast killer
Hewitt and Skelton are the Carriers
        And Holmes, Cammel and Shepherd the farriers
Mr Adlard's the Wesleyan Preacher
        Annie Pinning's a pupil teacher

Mr Broughton makes straps & traces
        Mr Simons likes going to races
Cuthert and Green both have mills
        Mr Parks deals in pills
James Bentley a man of great renown
        Keeps the only druggist shop in our town
He has all kinds of pills and drugs
        Also poison for killing bugs
At drawing teeth he shows much skill
        And he knows how to put things down in his bill
He has not much to bother his life
        And is seldom seen without his wife
Doctor Shearwood cures all ills
        By his medicines and pills
He also likes a drink and a smoke
        And often visits the "Royal Oak"
He has got a sister named Sarah Ann
        A lovely "maiden" say what you can
She is rather tall and sings in the choir
        And her face and nose are as red as a fire
Her brother caught her in the dairy one day
        But whether true I cannot say
She took a candle from the shelf
        And with it tried to hurt herself
She was often at Boyles when he was here
        But since he's gone she's shed may a tear
Home on a night Boyle did toil
        And so she got christened "2nd Mrs Boyle"
But now he has gone far away
        Let us hope she will get better some day
Hardy keeps a pork butcher's shop
        And his wife has the sausage meat to chop

His shop does such a roaring trade
        That upon poor pigs, he makes a good raid
There is a surgeon in Barrow called Philpot
        And he is the best doctor we have got
He only has one fault I think
        And that he is fond of drink
Susanah Smith plays on the organ
        Westoby's dress maker's Catherine Morgan
Old mother Brown sells all kinds of toys
        And her shop's often full of girls and boys
She is up to the mark in every trick
        But still she'll let people have things on tick
Mr West makes boots and shoes
        At Bentley's tannery they make glues
At the National School of lads and lasses
        Miss Travis teaches the first two classes
The rest of the scholars are sent spinning
        By Almena Westoby and Annie Pinning
Miss Hutton too, who comes from Beverley
        Teaches the infants very cleverly
Hewitt, 'tis said is a very good cobbler
        Young George Banks, is named "nobbler"
Arthur Belton has got a curious "walk"
        And with the girls he meets, will talk
Joshua Berry is a cunning old fellow
        And at church on a Sunday his bass he does bellow
Upon the cornet he likes to play
        And attends to his wife in every way
Timothy Brown keeps a grocers shop
        "Dolly" King is a regular fop
Dinah Kirby is a single woman
        And her son Jack is a rum-un

> She's got 4 more, it's curious rather
>> Pray can you tell me, "Who is the father?"
>
> This narrative I must now conclude
>> I trust you will not think me rude
> As I composed these lines at ease
>> I did it with intent to please
> Four years in Barrow I have been
>> And many of its people seen
> And if to these offence I've given
>> I only trust to be forgiven
> I must now conclude this poor oration
>> But hope it may meet with your approbation.

The parish of Holy Trinity Barrow now registers more than 5000 persons. It is a well-loved and thriving church, and not only because of the copy of the portrait of John Harrison greeting you on entry and the exhibition of his achievements alongside. The pupils at the nearby John Harrison Church of England Primary School can be seen out to play, clad in their deep blue sweat shirts embroidered with a commemorative badge of the illustrious village inhabitant. Overhead, is the distinctive weather vane designed by one of the scholars, Richard Pike in Year 6, when a competition was held for the pupils within the school in 1993 marking the 300th anniversary of the birth of John 'Longitude' Harrison, who himself won a recognition from King and Parliament for making the sea and world a much safer place.

No doubt he would be well pleased to know that it was manufactured* and painted** at Grimsby, which he knew well and then assembled by a parent and school governor, Jim Hackney of the village of Barrow upon Humber.

*D G Fabrications, Adam Smith Street, Grimsby
**David Allison, Art Teacher, Matthew Humberston School, Grimsby.

JOHN FLAMSTEED, FIRST ROYAL ASTRONOMER – A LIVING AT BURSTOW AND BOYHOOD IN DERBY

In 1685, when Lord North gave the living of the parish of St Bartholomew at Burstow on the Surrey-Sussex border to the thirty-nine year old John Flamsteed, it must have seemed like manna from heaven to the struggling astronomer at the Royal Observatory Greenwich trying to fund his equipment. The cost of this had not been mentioned in his briefings for the position he held; otherwise the two sets of orders issued within a period of three months by the monarch ten years previously.

WARRANT OF APPOINTMENT FROM CHARLES II TO THE OFFICERS OF HIS ORDNANCE THE COURT OF WHITEHALL 4TH MARCH 1675

"Whereas we have appointed our trusty and well-beloved John Flamsteed, Master of Arts, our Astronomical Observer, forthwith to apply himself with the most exact care and diligence to the rectifying the tables of the motions of the heavens, and the places of fixed stars, so as to find out the so much desired LONGITUDE of places, for the perfecting the art of NAVIGATION, and our will and pleasure is. and we do hereby require and authorise you, for the support and maintenance of the said John Flamsteed of whose ability in astronomy we have good testimony, and are well satisfied that, from time to time, you pay or cause to be paid to him, the said John Flamsteed, or his assigns the yearly salary or allowance of one hundred pounds; the same to be charged and borne upon the quarter books of the Office of Ordnance, and paid to him quarterly by even and equal portions, by the Treasurer of our said Office, the first quarter to begin and be accompted from the feast of ST MICHAEL THE ARCHANGEL, last past and so to continue during our pleasure. And for doing this shall be as well unto you, as to the Auditors of the Exchequer, for allowing the same,

and all other our officers and ministers whom it may concern, a full and sufficient warrant."

WARRANT OF APPOINTMENT FROM CHARLES II TO SIR THOMAS CHICHELEY, Knt MASTER OF ORDNANCE 22ND JUNE 1675

"Whereas in order to the finding out of the longitude of places for perfecting Navigation and Astronomy, we have resolved to build a small Observatory within our park at Greenwich, upon the highest ground, at or near the place where the Castle stood, with lodging rooms for our Astronomical Observator and assistant. Our will and pleasure is that according to such plot and design as shall be given you by our trusty and well- beloved Sir Christopher Wren, Knight, our Surveyor General of the place and scite of the said Observatory, you cause the same to be fenced in, built and finished with all convenient speed, by such artificers and workmen as you shall appoint thereto, and that you give order unto our Treasurer of the Ordnance for the paying of such materials and workmen as shall be used and employed therein out of such monies as shall come to your hand for old and decayed powder which hath or shall be sold by our order of the 1st January last, provided that the whole sum, so to be expended and paid, shall not exceed £500, and our pleasure is, that all our officers and servants belonging to our said Park be assisting to those that you shall appoint, for the doing thereof, and for so doing, this shall be to you and to all others whom it may concern a sufficient warrant."

John Flamsteed's appointment as the first Royal Astronomer could be said to have been all about being in the right place at the right time, otherwise that of being a guest in the apartment at the Tower of London allocated to the then Surveyor General of Ordnance, Sir Jonas Moore. It was spring 1675 and he was due to be ordained at Easter in London; his family had long associations with the clergy in his native Derbyshire.

Sir Jonas Moore quickly co-opted him onto the committee hastily set up to examine the possibility of calculating longitude by the stars and report back to the monarch who, is reputed to have commented, when informed of the inadequacy of the existing catalogues that he *'must have them anew observed, examined and corrected for the use of my seamen'.*

John Flamsteed's association with Sir Jonas Moore had begun several years previously with his compilation of an Astronomical Almanac. The year before he had printed his observations of a solar eclipse, having discovered that the current tables were considerably different from his own observations begun several years before on leaving school. Stricken with what has been thought rheumatic fever when aged fourteen, his formal teaching had been much interrupted so he studied mathematics and astronomy at home in Derby. It is now the opinion of Dr Peter Golding, also a Derbyshire local historian, that John Flamsteed possibly contracted Weil's disease, a very severe form of leptospirosis, when swimming in the River Derwent.

In 1669 the twenty-two year old John Flamsteed sent his Astronomical Almanac to the Royal Society in London. Because of their recognition of his son's work his father arranged for him to visit London. An introduction to Sir Jonas Moore ensued. The aspiring young astronomer was presented with a Towneley's micrometer and promised expensesd towards lenses for a telescope. En route home he stopped to see Isaac Newton in Cambridge and enrolled at the university. He gained his degree in 1674 and intended taking the living of a small parish in Derbyshire, gifted by a friend of his father's. His visit to London the following year changed all that. In 1676 he was elected a Fellow of the Royal Society.

There was little prestige to his appointment as Royal Astronomer, no grant for instruments and he was obliged to pay one tenth of his salary in tax, then calculated at £10 a year. He was also required to teach two boys from Christ's Hospital. It is estimated that during his long tenure of the position he would teach a total of 140 boys, many from well-to-do families.

Sir Jonas Moore initially came to his rescue with the provision of an iron sextant with a 7 ft radius; the two famous clocks by Tompion, a long telescope and some books followed. Unfortunately, his benevolent patron died in 1679 just four years after he began his life's work. Six years later came the death of the monarch and the gift of the living of Burstow; this would prove to be a lifeline and refuge for the weary and for many years cash-strapped pioneering scientist endeavouring to provide equipment from his own resources. There was no government aid for this or for repairs throughout his long tenure and the early years were very hard.

He succeeded as Rector from one Ralph Cooke whose widow died the following year. It is thought John Flamsteed met his future wife through these connections at Burstow. He would marry Margaret Cooke, grand-daughter of Ralph in 1692 at the Church of St Lawrence Jewry, in the City of London; her father was engaged at nearby Lincoln's Inn.

A rather different scenario to the 4,850 acres of isolated Sussex-Surrey border, comprising 'the ancient Wealden parish' of Burstow where John Flamsteed had by then well begun his stint of thirty-four years commuting the round trip of over sixty miles or so, to and from Greenwich. He journeyed there every six months, mainly on rough cart tracks and bridle paths, for a stay of approximately one week's duration until he died.

It is recorded that the 11th century church was then the focal point of a rural community surrounding four moated manor houses; the largest of these was the adjacent Burstow Court. The number of inhabitants in the region probably numbered just a few hundred. Here, however, John Flamsteed could enjoy much needed respite and attend to parish affairs personally. For communication he relied on the Penny Post and the General Post; his numerous letters on the administration during his absences were dealt with at Reigate and had to be collected from Horley.

He relied on curates; the cost of these swallowing up most of his stipend. However, he could claim Tithes and goods in kind which helped subsidise his rather economical existence at the Royal Observatory. Only the death of his father in 1688, several years before he married, enabled him to purchase a major and much needed instrument for the Royal Observatory. This cost £120 and he was promised reimbursement by the then Master of Ordnance, but this never materialised.

Stephen Flamsteed, a maltster and churchwarden at the now derelict St Werburgh's in Derby, appears to have been a man of some substance for he was able to finance his young son on an arduous month- long but fruitless trip to Ireland in search of health when he was nineteen. But it would be of no avail, John Flamsteed would suffer continuously from ill-health to the end of his life. A person, it seems, of great integrity and much respected by staff and family, affectionate but rendered irritable by his persistent afflictions. He was born at Denby near Derby in August 1646 where his parents had taken refuge from the plague; nearly half a century before the birth of John 'Longitude' Harrison in not so distant Yorkshire. They would later move back into Derby and enter their son for the free grammar school. This building is now the home of the Derbyshire Heritage Centre.

Stephen Flamsteed had known much tragedy. The weakly young John's mother died when he was just three years old and his father would be widowed yet again in 1854. Several other siblings did not survive childhood. His half sister, Katherine, would die in childbirth, leaving a niece, Anne. She would marry Jacob Hodgson, an assistant at the Royal Observatory and be joint executrix of her uncle's will.

John Flamsteed died at Greenwich on 31st January 1719, reportedly of 'strangury'. and was buried at Burstow a fortnight later. He left his wife £350 in ready money and £120 in Exchequer and South Sea Bonds plus another £50 per annum for personal use. He would also leave income from £25 for two coats for two poor old folk of the parish. When Margaret Flamsteed died in 1730 she was interred beside him in the chancel area. In turn, she bequeathed the income from £25 for two gowns and petticoats for two poor widows of the parish. They had no children, but a great nephew is known to have been the Reverend Richard Flamsteed, minister at Chellaston near Derby.

A memorial east window and a tablet near the chancel would be later be dedicated. Today the village of Burstow remembers him with pride. The Church Hall and a House Team in the local primary school are named after him. Faraway in Derbyshire, a Millenium Committee was set up in 2000 to celebrate his associations with the village of Denby; schoolchildren were involved in projects. A plaque was put up to mark the site of his birth in a long since demolished house named 'Crowtrees'; in the appropriately-named Flamsteed Lane about 500 yards south-east of Denby Church. The John Flamsteed Memorial Park in Denby Village was also established opposite the church. It is somewhat hard to understand that there is not a statue of John Flamsteed anywhere in the town of Derby, but the Derby Heritage staff are fervently hoping that this anomaly will soon be rectified.

Now in the skies above Burstow village, where the tired John Flamsteed chose to be buried in the peace of the Surrey countryside, the jet planes roar overhead en route worldwide from Gatwick Airport; using for direction the navigation systems that his devotion to accuracy in his calculations laid the foundations of several centuries ago, augmented by the discoveries of Isaac Newton of the accurate prediction of flight paths.

Maybe John Flamsteed would allow himself a wry smile at what might seem to be the seemingly persistent salutations from the heavens above applauding his efforts to determine safe travelling at sea, deduced from the movements of the stars on high and resulting in the advent of Greenwich Mean Time.

A–Z TIPS FOR TOURISTS AND VISITORS

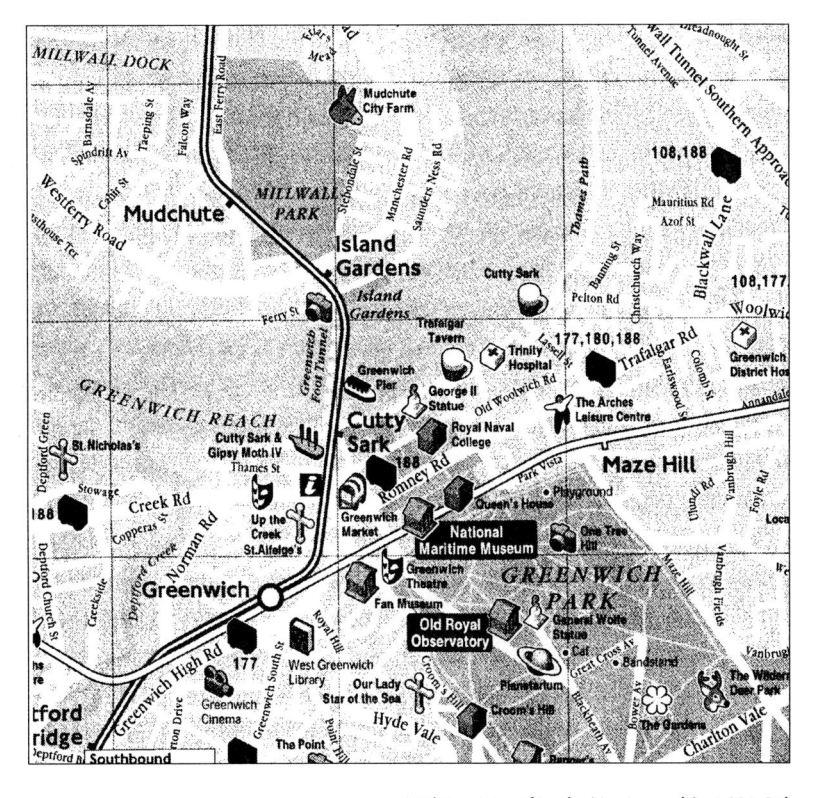

With permission of London Transport and Snap-Map Ltd

INDEX

SECTION 1

Visitors Centre – Tourist Information Office – Guided Walks
Access by Rail – Directions from Stations
Underground access
Docklands Light Railway
Access by Bus – From Central London & Lewisham
Local and Mobility
Access by Road & Parking
Shuttle Bus to Royal Observatory from Greenwich Pier
Access by River
City Airport – General Information – Shuttle Bus to Canary Wharf (DLR)

SECTION 2

National Maritime Museum – General information
Access by Road and Public Transport
Royal Observatory Greenwich General information
Access by Road and Public Transport (some disabled facilities)
Queen's House
Chapel and Painted Ceiling Old Royal Naval College
(some disabled facilities)
Cutty Sark (some disabled facilities)

SECTION 3

Island Gardens and Foot Tunnel
Ranger's House
Fan Museum
Greenwich Theatre   **Meridian Clock Tower**
St Alfege Church   **Greenwich Market**

Goddards Pie House
The Yacht Inn
Queen Elizabeth's College Almshouses
Trinity Hospital
Master Shipwright's House, Deptford
Royal Artillery Museums Ltd (Royal Arsenal) Woolwich
Charlton House
Eltham Palace
Thames Barrier
HMS Belfast
National Maritime Museum, Cornwall
John Harrison in Lincolnshire – Barrow on Humber – Brocklesby Park
John Flamsteed – A Living at Burstow, Surrey, and Boyhood in Derby
British Horological Institute
Clock Room, Guildhall, London
British Museum
Science Museum
Natural History Museum
Useful Addresses and Telephone Numbers

Trafalgar Tavern
Cutty Sark Tavern

Golden Hind
Shakespeare's Globe Theatre

SECTION 1

Greenwich Gateway:
WORLD HERITAGE SITE VISITORS CENTRE,
Pepys House, Old Royal Naval College, Cutty Sark Gardens, London SE10 9LW

Greenwich Gateway freephone: 0800 389 3341

www.greenwichfoundation.org.uk

Tiltyard Café and Toilets

GREENWICH TOURIST INFORMATION CENTRE
(General Enquiries) Pepys House, Cutty Sark Gardens, London SE10 9LW

Tel: 0870 608 2000 Fax: 020 8853 4607

E-mail: tic@greenwich.gov.uk

GREENWICH TOUR GUIDES ASSOCIATION
Tel: 020 8858 6169 Fax: 020 8244 3013

E-mail: gmcooper@excite.com

Royal Greenwich Meridian Walk commences at Tourist Information Centre. Daily 12.15 and 14.15.

DIRECTIONS FROM GREENWICH STATION
Daily service approx 20 -30 min from Charing Cross and London Bridge Stations (Cannon Street Mon-Sat)

Leave by main exit and turn left onto Greenwich High Road; Ten-minute stroll will bring you to town centre and National Maritime Museum.

Bus No 177 leaves from outside station and Nos. 180 and 199 can be joined nearby in Greenwich High Road.

UNDERGROUND

Tel: 020 7222 1234 Minicom: 020 7918 3015
Jubilee Line: Mon–Sat: 05.05 – 00.41 Sun: 07.04 – 23.52
Operates from Stanmore in North London via Baker Street, Bond Street, Green Park, Westminster, Waterloo, Southwark, London Bridge, Canada Water and from Stratford in East London via West Ham and Canning Town to Canary Wharf.
Connect at Canary Wharf with Docklands Light Railway.

DOCKLANDS LIGHT RAILWAY

Tel: 020 7222 1234
Minicom: 020 7918 3015
Docklands Travel Hotline (24 hours): 020 7918 4000
DLR Customer Services: 020 7363 9700
E-mail: Customer Services at cservice@dir.co.uk. www.dir.co.uk.
Operates from Bank Underground Station (Central Line) in the City, Tower Gateway (District and Circle Lines to Tower Hill) and Stratford in East London to Canary Wharf, then on to Lewisham via Heron Quays, South Quay, Cross Harbour and London Arena, Mudchute, Island Gardens, Cutty Sark for Maritime Greenwich, Greenwich, Deptford Bridge and Elverson Road.

BUSES TO GREENWICH

No 188: Russell Square > Waterloo > Nth Greenwich.
Stops by Cutty Sark Gardens. Journey (approx 1 hour).
No 53: Oxford Circus > New Cross > Blackheath Hill > Plumstead
Stops on Charlton Way for Royal Observatory Greenwich (approx 1 hour).
No 180: Lewisham > Greenwich > Woolwich >Thamesmead East.
Stops in Romney Road outside National Maritime Museum
No 199: Catford >Lewisham > Greenwich > Canada Water
Stops at South Street, Greenwich, for mainline station & DLR.
Stops at Church Street for Cutty Sark Gardens.

LOCAL BUSES South East Daily

No 177: Peckham > Greenwich (main station, DLR, Cutty Sark) > Thamesmead.

No 286: Greenwich (Cutty Sark, DLR) > Eltham > Sidcup.

No 386: Greenwich (Cutty Sark, DLR) > Shooters Hill > Woolwich.

Nos. 54: Woolwich > Blackheath > Elmers End

202: Blackheath > Crystal Palace

380: Lewisham > Blackheath > Shooters Hill > Woolwich Arsenal.

MOBILITY BUSES

No 851/852: Greenwich > Bromley North Station (Mon)

No 853: Greenwich > Bromley Hospital, Mason's Hill (off High Street) (Fri)

Access & Mobility, Transport for London, Windsor House, 42-50 Victoria Street, London SW1H 0TL

Tel/Text: 020 7941 4600 Fax: 020 7941 4605

ROAD ROUTES TO GREENWICH

Approx 30 minutes from Central London and 1-2 hours from Dover and Channel ports.

A206 Romney Road runs outside the National Maritime Museum through the Greenwich Heritage Site and is 1 mile (1.6 Km) from the Blackwall Tunnel.

A2 (Blackheath Hill), A20, South Circular, M11.

M25 via A2 junction or A13/A102 Blackwall Tunnel .

The Royal Observatory and Planetarium border Blackheath Avenue, entered via Blackheath Gate on Charlton Way and can also be reached from the town centre via King William Walk and The Avenue in Greenwich Park, or by Maze Hill to the east.

CAR PARKING

Very limited space in town centre. Pay and Display in Burney Street (by cinema) & Park Row (off Romney Rd).

Space may be available in NMM Staff Car Park in Park Row (off Romney Rd) at weekends only. Parking meters.
PARKING IN GREENWICH PARK (closed daily at dusk to 07.00)
Police and Parks Office Tel: 020 7262 8878
Pay and Display 09.00 – 18.00. Maximum stay 4 hours.

SHUTTLE BUS: GREENWICH PIER TO ROYAL OBSERVATORY

The Meridian Line Shuttle-Bus Service operates daily from Greenwich Pier starting at approx 10.00 during April-Oct, at 15-minute intervals. Journey to the Royal Observatory approx 10 minutes via Greenwich Park.
Seasonal restrictions. Enquiries to Tourist Information Centre.

ACCESS BY RIVER THAMES

City Cruises **Tel**: 020 7740 0400/020 7930 9033
www.citycruises.com. Operate between Westminster, Waterloo, Tower and Greenwich Piers.
Service from Westminster to Greenwich starts at 10.20 and takes approx 1 hour. The last return boat leaves Greenwich Pier around 17.45 (earlier in winter).
Greenwich Pier to Thames Barrier. Daily (excluding January) **Tel**: 020 8305 0300
For other operators and further information:
The River Thames Boat Service Guide can be obtained from: London River Services Ltd, Tower Millennium Pier, Lower Thames Street, London EC3N 4DT.
Tel: 020 7941 2400.

CITY AIRPORT

Passenger Terminal, Royal Docks, London E16 2PX.
Admin: Civil Aviation House, London City Airport, Royal Docks, E16 2PB. (contd)

CITY AIRPORT (cont.)

Tel: 020 7646 0088/07000 CITY AIRPORT
E-mail: info@londoncityairport.com
www.londoncityairport.com for on line bookings

Shuttle Bus Service to Liverpool Street Station (Bus Stop A) **via Canary Wharf (North Colonnade) for DLR connection to Greenwich** (Timetable 020 7646 0088).

SECTION 2

THE NATIONAL MARITIME MUSEUM (NMM)

ADDRESS: Romney Road, Greenwich, London SE10 9NF
TEL: 020 8858 4422
RECORDED INFORMATION: Tel: 020 8312 6565
FAX: 020 8312 6632 www.nmm.ac.uk
OPEN: Daily 10.00 – 18.00 June – Sept (10.00 – 1700 Oct – May)
Last admission half an hour before closing.
(Buses 177, 180, 188, 286, 386, N1 stop outside)
CLOSED: Dec 24 – 26
INFORMATION DESK inside main entrance by shop.
Toilets (disabled) on all levels.
Places to Eat: Snack Bar on Level 2 and Regatta Café (also entered from park).
Braille Guides. Touch Talks and Tours. Lifts all levels.
Friends 020 8312 6678.
ADMISSION FREE excepting special exhibitions

THE ROYAL OBSERVATORY GREENWICH (including Planetarium)

ADDRESS, TEL, FAX, E-MAIL: As for National Maritime Museum.
WEBSITE: www.rog.nmm.ac.uk
Flamsteed Astronomy Society Tel: 020 8312 6678
E-mail: friends@nmm.ac.uk
Deaf Astronomy Society Tel: 020 8312 6740
OPENING HOURS As for NMM.
Open evenings for special events.
(Bus no 53 to Charlton Way or shuttle bus from pier or walk up through park)
See Parking in Greenwich Park.
FREE ADMISSION except Planetarium and special events.

(cont.)

THE ROYAL OBSERVATORY (cont.)

Some areas not feasible for disabled due to age of building (toilet facilities).

Park Café opposite.

PLANETARIUM Shows available most weekday afternoons. Tel: 020 8312 6608 to check times and details of weekend openings.

THE QUEEN'S HOUSE

ADDRESS, TEL, FAX, WEBSITE & OPENING HOURS
as for NMM

ENTRANCE – Facing Romney Road. Level to undercroft area. Suitable for Disabled. Lifts inside to all floors.

INFORMATION DESK – just inside entrance. Audio guides and floor plans available etc. Cloakroom and Toilets adjacent. No eating facilities.

ADMISSION FREE (except special events)

GROUND FLOOR
Great Hall

Special Exhibitions, (Artist-in-residence), Orangery.

Historic Greenwich Exhibition

Models of the house, Early landscapes, Stuart portraits.

The Tudors at Greenwich Exhibition

Tudor portraits, Armada, Education: Face to Face.

FIRST FLOOR
Great Hall and Gallery

Conservation Studio, Loggia

Exhibition Space in the Centre Bridge Rooms, the former King's and Queen's Presence Chambers, Bed Chambers, Ante Rooms, Privy Chambers etc.

THE ROYAL HOSPITAL CHAPEL AND PAINTED DINING HALL
(OLD ROYAL NAVAL COLLEGE)

ADDRESS: The Greenwich Foundation, Old Royal Naval College, Greenwich, London SE10 9LW

LOCATION: adjacent to Visitors Centre alongside the Cutty Sark Gardens.

TEL: 020 8269 4747 **FREEPHONE** 0800 389 3341

FAX: 020 8269 4757 www.greenwichfoundation.org.uk

OPEN: Mon-Sat 10.00 – 17.00 Sun 12.30 – 17.00 (last visitor 16.15)

CLOSED: 24 – 26 December

(Buses stopping outside 177,180, 188,286,386 N1)

Places to eat (not Saturdays): Queen Mary Ante-room Snack Bar and Wardroom Restaurant (menu £14 - £24 [2003]). Toilet facilities. Some access for disabled. Guide Dogs.

Admission free

THE CUTTY SARK

ADDRESS: King William Walk, Greenwich, London SE10 9HT

TEL: 020 8858 3445 **FAX**: 020 8853 3445 www.cutttysark.org.uk

OPEN: Daily 10.00 – 18.00 April-Sept (17.00 winter)

Guided Tours by arrangement. Reduced rates for parties booked in advance. Guide to charges: Family Ticket £9.80 (2003). Groups of 10+ (20% discount)

CLOSED: Dec 24 – 26

Wheelchair access to 'tween deck only. Nearest other facilities in Visitor Centre.

The Maritime Trust, Ship Preservation Charity, Greenwich Church Street, London SE10 9BG. Tel: 020 8858 2698. Fax: 020 8853 3589

SECTION 3

ISLAND GARDENS AND THE GREENWICH FOOT TUNNEL

Location: Walk from Cutty Sark Gardens – entry by Greenwich Pier.
FREE
OPEN Mon – Sat 07.00 – 19.00 Sun 10.00 – 17.30

RANGER'S HOUSE HISTORICAL MUSEUM

Chesterfield Walk, Greenwich, London SE10 8QX Tel: 020 8853 0035
Location: Top of Croom's Hill near junction with Blackheath Hill/Charlton Way, bordering bowling green near south west perimeter of Greenwich Park.
Approx 10 -15 min stroll from Royal Observatory.

THE FAN MUSEUM

12 Croom's Hill, Greenwich, London SE10 8ER
Tel: 020 8858 7879/020 8305 1441 Fax: 020 8293 1889
Location: Near the bottom of Croom's Hill. On the right if approaching from the town via Stockwell Street off Greenwich Church Street.
OPEN: Tues – Sat 11.00 – 17.00 Sun 12.00 – 17.30
CLOSED: Monday (except by arrangement)

GREENWICH THEATRE

Croom's Hill, London SE10 8ES
Tel: 020 8858 7755 24 hour booking www.greenwichtheatre.org.uk
Location: Bottom of Croom's Hill at the junction of Nevada Street, opposite Burney Street; three-minute walk from Greenwich Church Street via Stockwell Street.
Box Office: Mon–Sat 10.00–20.00
Sun/Bank Holiday One hour before performances.

ST ALFEGE CHURCH

Greenwich Church Street, London SE10
Tel: 020 8293 5595 / 020 8853 2703 / 020 8858 6828
www.stalfege.org.
Open: Mon-Sat 10.00 – 16.00 Sun 12.00 – 1700.
Visitors welcome to come in quietly during Sunday and other services.

GREENWICH MARKET

approached by cobbled lanes from town centre or by colonnaded entrance in College Approach
Tel: 020 7515 7153 (Wed – Sun 020 8293 3110)
OPEN: Seven days a week.
Wed/Fri/Sat/Sun Arts and Crafts 09.30 – 17.30.
Thurs Antiques and Collectables 09.00 – 17.00.
Fri Farmers Market Sat & Sun Food Fair

GODDARD'S PIE HOUSE

45 Church Street, Greenwich, London SE10 9BL
Licensed. Est. 1890
Tel: 020 8293 9313 (Parties welcome) www.pieshop.co.uk
Location: Opposite Greenwich Market by Cutty Sark Gardens
OPEN: Mon – Thurs 10.00 – 18.30 Fri, Sat, Sun 10.00 – 21.30

TRAFALGAR TAVERN

Park Row SE 10
Tel: 020 8858 2437
Dining Room Sun 12.00 – 1600 Mon 12.00 – 15.00 Tues-Sat 12.00 – 21.00
Location: On riverfront. Three minute walk from East Gate of the Old Roy Naval Coll.
Accessible on foot by Thames Path and by car to Park Row.

The Cutty Sark Tavern

4-6 Ballast Quay, East Greenwich SE10 9PD
Tel: 020 8858 3146
Location: On riverfront. Five to ten minute walk from the Trafalgar Tavern along the Thames Path beyond Trinity Hospital and the Electric Power Station.
Accessible by car from Lassell Street, off Trafalgar Road.

Queen Elizabeth's College Almshouses

Greenwich High Road, London SE 10.
Tel: 020 8858 2852
Location: The large lawn with central chapel, surrounded by immaculate cottages, can be easily identified on the right hand side opposite the mainline station.

Trinity Hospital

High Bridge Road, London SE 10.
Warden Tel: 020 8858 1310
Location: On riverbank, downriver from the Trafalgar Tavern and nestling beneath the giant black chimneys of the Electric Power Station. The white-painted miniature-battlemented façade can be easily identified from Island Gardens.

Master Shipwright's House

Watergate Street, Deptford, London SE 8
Tel: 0208 692 5836
Location: Deptford mainline station (one stop from Greenwich). Turn left outside and walk down Deptford High Street, cross Evelyn Street and Watergate Street is almost opposite. Walk down to end to Twinkle Park. Roof visible beyond large iron gates.
Open for arts events and exhibitions (see London Open House)
Further info on e-mail: willishipwrights@yahoo.com (contact: Mr William Richards)

The Royal Artillery Museums Ltd

Old Laboratory Office, Royal Arsenal, Woolwich, London SE18 6ST
Tel: 020 8855 7755 (Recorded Information)
Fax: 020 8855 7100
E-mail: info@firepower.org.uk www.firepower.org.uk
Open Daily 10.00 – 17.00 (last admission 16.00)
Closed 25 December.
Charge for admission (under review) Family ticket £18 (2002)
Location:
Rail: Woolwich Arsenal Station is five stops beyond Greenwich mainline station.
Road: just off the A2 and South Circular (A 205), near Woolwich Ferry.
Ample parking for cars and coaches. Well signposted.
Buses: No 53 from Central London (see as for Royal Observatory) Otherwise Nos. 54, 472, 161, 180, 380, 422.
Underground: Jubilee Line to North Greenwich, then Buses 161, 422, 472.

Charlton House

Charlton Road, Charlton, London SE7 8RE.
Tel: 020 8856 3951
Fax: 020 8856 4162
www.greenwich.council.gov.uk
Open as Community Centre and Library Mon – Fri 09.00 – 22.00. Weekends – Private Hire. Licensed Bar.
Viewing by appointment. Grounds open to public.

Eltham Palace & Gardens

Court Yard, Eltham, London SE 9.
Tel: 0208 294 2548
Open Wed – Friday, Sundays and Bank Holiday Mondays throughout year. (contd)

Eltham Palace & Gardens (cont.)
Apr - Sept 10.00-18.00 October 10.00-17.00 Nov - Mar 10.00-16.00
Location:
Rail: Charing Cross and Victoria direct to Eltham (Well Hall Road)
Road: Junction 3 on M25 and then A20 to Eltham, off Court Road From Central London: A2.
Buses: to Eltham Parish Church (High Street) Nos. 124, 126, 160, 161, 286, 321.

Thames Barrier Information Centre
1 Unity Way, Woolwich, London SE 18 5NJ. **Tel**: 020 8305 4188
Open Daily except 24 December – 1 January
Public exhibition, open every day, 10.30am - 4.30pm, 31 March - 29 Sept; 11.00am-3.30pm; 30 Sept - 30 March. Free viewing of Flood Barrier always possible from riverbank except during very bad weather; programme of days when checking gates obtainable in advance: www.environment.agency.gov.uk
Location:
Road: via A206 Woolwich Road. **Rail**: Charlton Station (15 min. walk).
Tube North Greenwich. **Buses**: 161, 177, 180, 472 to Woolwich Road

The *Golden Hinde*
St Mary Overie Dock, Cathedral Street, London SE1 9DE
Open Daily. Admission Charge Tel: 020 7403 0123 & 0870 011 87. Please phone before visiting to check opening times as special events may be taking place occasionally.
Location: Rail/Underground/Bus to London Bridge (five min. walk)

HMS *Belfast*
Morgans Lane, Tooley Street, London SE1 2JH
Open Daily (except 24-26 Dec) Admission Charge
Recorded Information: 020 7940 6300 **Fax**: 020 7403 0719
Location: Rail/Underground/Bus to London Bridge (three min. walk)

Shakespeare's Globe

New Globe Walk, Bankside, London SE1 9DT
Exhibition Tel: 020 7902 1500
Box Office Tel: 0200 7401 9919
Main Tel: 020 7902 1400 Fax 020 7902 1401
Restaurant Tel: 020 7928 9444
Location: South bank of Thames between Blackfriars and Southwark Bridges.
Underground: 1) London Bridge 2) Blackfriars across the river (Five to ten minutes along riverbank) 3) Mansion House and walk over Southwark Bridge (Five to ten minutes). Also Southwark (Jubilee Line) and Cannon Street.
Buses: Numerous routes and services available from central London area (RV1 to and from Covent Garden)

THE NATIONAL MARITIME MUSEUM CORNWALL

(An independent charitable trust supported by the Heritage Lottery Fund and other agencies)
Address: Discovery Quay, Falmouth, Cornwall TR11 3QY
Tel: 01326 313388. **Fax:** 01326 317878
e-mail: enquiries@nmmc.co.uk. **Web:** www.nmmc.co.uk
Location: Eastern end of Falmouth Harbour between docks and waterfront. Admission Charge. Families £15.50 (2003) 12 state-of-the-art Galleries. Focuses on evolution of boats mainly over the last two centuries for work and recreation with particular reference to Cornwall's maritime history. A collection of some 150 craft will be on show in annual rotas of specific interest from the National Small Boat Collection donated by NMMGreenwich.
Other Facilities: Lecture Theatre (100 seats). Library with 12,000 books and interactive technology, Education Centre, Shop and Restaurant. Waterside piazza accommodate up to 4,000.
Access By Road: A39 to Falmouth and follow signs.
Train: 300 metres from Falmouth Town Station.

JOHN HARRISON IN LINCOLNSHIRE

Cleethorpes Tourist Information Office, 42-43 Alexandra Road, Cleethorpes DN35 8LE
Tel 01472 323 111
Fax 01472 323 112

Barrow upon Humber Location:

By road A 1107 (B 1206) (Barton upon Humber and Humber Bridge A15).

By bus Service 250 from Grimsby (Mon-Sat) Approx one hour.

By rail to Barrow Haven and short walk to village (approx 10 mins).

By air to Humberside International. Tel: 01652 688456/682068. (connect Barnetby)

www.nelines.gov.uk

Holy Trinity Church, Barrow upon Humber Tel 01469 530 357
Thornton Curtis Church where John Harrison also worked and records survive reached as for Thornton Abbey Tel 01652 657 053 (Road and bus as for Barrow upon Humber)

Local resident and worker in stoneware *sgriffto* tiles of John Harrison's cottage:
Mr J Amos, 'Santos', Wold Road, Barrow upon Humber, North Lincs, DN19 7BT Tel 01469 530 246

Local artist who supplies paintings of John Harrison's cottage:
Gordon Broadwith, High Barnes, Barton Street, Barrow upon Humber,

Brocklesby Park for John Harrison's Turret Clock viewed by arrangement: Apply to Earl of Yarborough's Estate Office, Brocklesby Park, Grimsby, DN41 8PN. **Tel:** 01469 560 214. **Fax:** 01469 561346. **E-mail:** office@brocklesby-estate.co.uk

JOHN FLAMSTEED AT BURSTOW, SURREY

Parish Church of St Bartholomew, Burstow
The Rectory, 5 The Acorns, Smallfield, Horley, Surrey RH6 9QV
Tel 01342 842224

Derby

Tourist Information Centre
Assembly Rooms
Market Place
Derby DE1 3AH
Tel: 01332 255802 **Fax:** 01332 256137
www.visitderby.co.uk

Derby Local Studies Library
Tel: 01332 255393 **Fax:** 01332 255381

Derby Heritage Centre (Richard Felix)
Old Tudor Hall
St Peter's Church
Derby DE1 1NN
Tel: 01332 299321

John Flamsteed Memorial Park
Denby Village (opp. church).
Approx. five miles from Derby city centre. Bus service.
Info: Reg Whitmarsh, Amber Valley Borough Council.
Tel: 01773 570222
www.ambervalley.gov.uk

The British Horological Institute

Tel: 01636 813 795

The Clockmakers' Company Collection of Clocks & Watches

Clock Room, Guildhall Library, Aldermanbury, London EC2.
Tel: 020 7606 3030
Admission FREE Mon-Fri
Underground: St Paul's

British Museum
Great Russell Street, London WC1B 3DG
General Enquiries: 020 7636 1555
Fax: 020 7323 8480
Admission FREE
Underground: Holborn, Tottenham Court Road, Russell Square

Science Museum
Exhibition Road, London SW7
Tel: Switchboard 020 7942 4000.
Recorded Information 020 7942 4998
Admission FREE
Underground: South Kensington

Natural History Museum
Cromwell Road, London SW7 5BD
Tel: (Recorded Information) 020 7942 5000
www.nhm.ac.uk
Admission FREE
Underground: South Kensington

Victoria & Albert Museum
Cromwell Road, London SW7 2RL
Tel: 020 7942 2528
Recorded Information 020 7942 2000
Admission FREE
Underground: South Kensington

APPENDICES

A FEW PARISHIONERS OF GREENWICH AND VISITOR PETER THE GREAT

St Alfege Church will tell you about some of the inhabitants and history of the town. A five-minute video, well-stocked shop and easy to follow guided trail has much to offer the visitor. The traffic-stained exterior belies a spacious interior of great tranquillity and interest. It is built on the site of the martyrdom of the 29th Archbishop of Canterbury who, in 1012, refused to allow a ransom of £3000 to be paid by his impoverished parishioners to the Danes.

The present building, extensively fire-damaged in WWII and rededicated in 1953, was designed by Nicholas Hawksmoor as 'English Baroque' with an oval ceiling suspended by tie-beams when the second church on the site collapsed in 1710. Parliament was petitioned for funding because so many of the residents were seamen, or their widows. The post-war restoration has faithfully followed his beautiful design and appropriate timbers for the ceiling were obtained from Hungerford in Berkshire.

The baptism of Henry VIII is commemorated in a window and wall tablets record the worship of the Royal Astronomers John Flamsteed, Sir George Biddell Airy and Sir Frank Dyson, who mooted the six-pip Greenwich Time Signal in 1924. General Gordon of Khartoum was a local resident and benefactor. The church organ was built by Messrs Spurden Rutt as a permanent memorial to Thomas Tallis, 'the father of English Church music'. He is believed to have used the organ installed in 1552; the probable console of which can be seen in the south-west corner today. Some of the keyboard of this is believed original; it is possible that two Queens of England, when the young princesses Mary and Elizabeth Tudor, played on it when they lived nearby at Greenwich Palace.

Buried in the vaults are General Wolfe of Quebec and Sir John

Angerstein of Lloyds, whose art collection was bought for the nation by Lord Liverpool and became the nucleus of the National Gallery when formed in 1824. Sir John Angerstein was sent to England from St Petersburg when a young boy to work in the City. Reputedly, his parentage is shrouded in obscurity; possibly born to a Russian lady of noble birth perhaps related to Czar Peter, he was put in the care of the German doctor who attended the confinement and took his surname. His beautiful former home at Woodlands in Mycenae Road, beyond Greenwich Park to the east, is now part community centre, art gallery and reference library.

Czar Peter was himself, for a few months in 1698, a visitor to Greenwich when on his *'embassy'* or fact-finding tour in 1698 as the sometimes incognito Peter Mikhailov. Czar since the age of ten, he studied and worked at the Royal Naval Docks at Deptford, enhancing his already considerable knowledge of mathematics and navigation. Visiting the Royal Observatory, the eager student by then in his early twenties and who had apparently been allowed a somewhat unrestricted upbringing with the frequent indulgence of noisy games, managed to damage property to the value of £27 12 sh 6d. A mortified John Flamsteed recorded the breakages of his clocks.

The reported frequently paralytic Czar Peter, over two metres tall and of exceptional strength, together with his comrade chums and it is suggested, the future Astronomer Royal Edmund Halley, also indulged in wild wheelbarrow races in the cherished garden of Sir John Evelyn's home, Sayes Court. The beautiful house which had been made available to the Russian entourage was systematically 'trashed'. The King's Surveyor, Sir Christopher Wren, was called in and listed over seventy dreadful instances of vandalism by the 'Zar of Muskovie'. A formidable estimate of £350 9sh 6d for repairs was presented to the Treasury. The devastated owner received compensation within a month from the Admiralty.

However, such was the importance of Russia in European affairs, that King William III gave Czar Peter his best yacht, the *Royal*

Standard, in which to sail back to Archangel as soon as the ice melted. Sixty master craftsmen travelled back with him to ply their skills in his country. The monarch also commissioned Sir Godfrey Kneller to paint the portrait of the young miscreant and reputedly received in return a large uncut diamond rolled up in dirty paper.

Also accorded an honorary degree in law from Oxford University, Czar Peter was prevailed upon by William Penn to attend some Quaker meetings at a house in the area of Deptford High Street. Mercifully, suitable decorum was preserved during the proceedings in which much interest was taken by the young czar, noting the contrast to the Russian Orthodox Church.

When Czar Peter died nearly three decades later many attributes would be accorded his reign, including the more favourable ones of statesmanship, zealous reforming, an ability to work skilfully at humble tasks and a preference for loose comfortable clothing suitable for manual labour when not obliged to wear formal attire. When Czar Peter visited England there was no navy in Russia.

When he died there was not only a large shipbuilding industry but also a Baltic Fleet with a complement of 28,000 personnel. He died in 1725 of a fever; reputedly contracted a few months earlier as a result of leaping into freezing water and assisting in the night-long rescue of some 20 sailors from a grounded ship.

His life-size bronze statue erected recently on Millenium Creek, Deptford, shows him in regal uniform and standing commandingly on a large plinth supplied from a Russian quarry. Framed by a backdrop of luxury flats, he looks downriver to Greenwich. The impressive monument was donated in 2001 by the Russian sculptor, Mikhail Cheniakin.

The location can easily be reached from Greenwich; it is about 10 minutes walk up Creek Road that leads off the Cutty Sark Gardens or two stops on the bus from Greenwich Church Street. It is also easily accessible from Deptford, via Evelyn Street, on foot or by bus from the present Sayes Court development of municipal homes now on the site where Sir John Evelyn lived from 1652-94 and where he wrote his now famous diary.

The Royal Dock at Deptford was then a 30-acre area (12 hectares) of world renown for its output of naval vessels. The five slipways, single and double dry docks would, in their time, service Drake's *Golden Hinde* and equip Captain Cook's *Resolution, Adventure* and *Discovery*.

THE THAMES FLOOD BARRIER

Since 1982 this magnificent structure, standing sentinel just 6 miles (9 Km) from London Bridge, has been the capital's very own impregnable 'sea wall'. The combined engineering and architectural genius of its construction ensures that the Upper Thames can be effectively sealed off from huge surge tides, caused by freak meteorological conditions of increasing intensity; exacerbated by the sea level rising relative to land at the rate of approximately two feet (60 cm) per century.

The first sighting is of the gleaming iridescent shell-contoured pier hoods, seemingly scale-covered and resembling upturned keels, straddling the river at Woolwich Reach; near the site of the old Royal Docks and where the river is relatively straight and about a third of a mile wide (500 m). The piers support six normally submerged mighty floodgates, designed as cellular structures and steel-plated to a thickness of 1.6 inches (4 cm).

Ever ready to be raised in emergency, the gates rest on massive curved concrete sills set in foundations sunk 55 ft (17 m) below in the chalk and flint river bed. To confront a dangerously rising water level, each gate pivots through ninety degrees from horizontal to vertical. The project was designed by the consulting engineer, Charles Draper; chosen from forty-one submissions. The cost of building was half a million pounds and a workforce of 4,000 was employed.

Run by the Environment Agency, the Barrier is assiduously controlled round-the-clock by approximately eighty personnel, working in shifts using state-of-the-art technology from the Central Control Room at the top of a ten-storey tower. From here, all the mustard-yellow operating machinery is always visible to the staff on duty. Each gate operates independently, power supplies come from three separate sources and controls are duplicated with fail-safe provision. The computer receives data direct from the Meteorological

Office over two independent landlines. There is usually a twelve-hour warning of a dangerous surge tide and a complete work-team can be at their posts within one hour of call out.

The operating sequence and speed has been calculated to cause minimum interference with the normal flow of the river. First the three falling radial gates on the north bank and the single one on the south bank, then the six great main gates starting from the outside; the two in the centre being the last to close. Action to close the Barrier is taken about one hour after low tide, five hours before an incoming surge tide could reach this point. Alongside on the south bank, which is constructed as a reinforced defence with a core of steel, are the generating house, workshops and Conference and Information Centre. Routine monthly testing of the gates rising is programmed well in advance and can be readily obtained. The conference facilities are also available for hire. (See Tips for Tourists)

HMS BELFAST

Pro Tanto Quid Retribuamus

(For so much how shall we repay?)

Nearby the City Pier and riding gently on the tides in the Pool of London, the stretch of water about half a nautical mile in length between London Bridge and Tower Bridge, this valiant steely-blue veteran cruiser now enjoys permanent anchorage; the big port guns silently focus on the adjacent revitalised Hay's Wharf. A short walk up the gangway onto her quarterdeck will bring you into shipboard intimacy of another era. Since sailing proudly up the Thames and opening to the public on Trafalgar Day 1971, having been saved for the nation by devotees, she survives as a floating museum and living memorial of life at sea in war and peace during the 20th century.

This remarkable vessel is now a long way from the oceans and 50 ft waves (15 m) that once swept over her great armoured hull as she steamed some half a million miles (800,000 Km) in war and peace, on operational duties for nearly thirty years. During hostilities she would carry a complement of over 900 officers and men. With a standard displacement of 11,553 tons, a length of 613 ft (187 m), a beam of 69 ft (21 m) and a draught of 20 ft (6 m), her unit propulsion engineering system provided a maximum speed of 32 knots (58 Km) per hour.

Now she is the only proud survivor of a famous fleet with the added distinction of being the first Royal Naval ship to be preserved since Nelson's *HMS Victory*, on view at Portsmouth, Hampshire, UK. Costing over £2 million pounds, launched in 1938 as a heavily-fortified flagship and severely mined not long after commissioning, *HMS Belfast* joined the perilous Arctic convoys in 1942 supplying essentials to Russia.

Boxing Day 1943 found her very actively participating in the Battle of North Cape, raging for eleven hours in the icy seas off Norway, resulting in the sinking of the 32,000 ton German battlecruiser, the *Scharnhorst*. It would be the last big gun battle at sea in Europe. The following year the D-Day landings in Normandy, then repatriation duties in the Far East, service with the UN in the Korean War, peacekeeping, a final visit to the city of Belfast and then three years as harbour accommodation at Devonport until 1966.

With decommissioning and scrapping a constant threat, a former captain decided to save her for posterity. After many struggles, Rear-Admiral Sir Morgan-Giles succeeded in 1971. When exploring *HMS Belfast*, conveniently divided into eight zones on seven decks, you are left in no doubt how this great ship functioned. From Galley to Chapel the attention to detail is meticulous and occasionally suitably humorous. Video monitors provide excellent background information and guidance.

THE GOLDEN HINDE

Previously known as *The Pelican* and built along Venetian lines as a 16th century wooden sailing ship, the historically authentic and fully operational replica of the original *Golden Hinde* can be visited in the small and tranquil St Mary Overie Dock; a stone's throw from Southwark Cathedral by London Bridge. She was commissioned by a company in San Francisco during the 1960s and on completion in 1973 sailed to California for commemorative celebrations. Archives record that the Bay of San Francisco is described as Port Sir Francis Drake in 1578; the Spaniards later took over.

The distinguished naval architect, Loring Christian Norgaard, an American of Norwegian descent, would bring his very considerable expertise and acumen to the Herculean task of the reconstruction; completed during 1971-73 by the Hinks Shipyard at Appledore in Devon, near Drake's birthplace in south-west England. Loring Norgaard would spend much time studying the 16th century manuscripts, for the shipbuilders of that period worked solely by ratios of length to depth and width; the craftsmen handed on their trades by virtue of hands, feet, arms and yards.

The only concessions to modernity are that the planking was laid with African iroko, for many of England's finest forests were laid bare forever in the shipbuilding effort required to defeat the Spanish Armada in 1588, and that a wheel was installed for safety in place of the original whip staff – merely a pole attached to the rudder. A fir tree of sufficient height for the present great mainmast was eventually found, after much searching nationwide, not far from where Drake lived at Buckland Abbey in Devon; now partly a museum it contains a few items of furniture fashioned from the remains of the original. This *Golden Hinde*, however, has not only circumnavigated the world following Drake's route but also visited 300 ports. She has sailed over 140,000 miles (225,300 Km); crewed only by a Master, Mate, Cook and a dozen deckhands in authentic costume. In Drake's day there were at least sixty crew who were sworn to secrecy; punishment was hard, as was life aboard, particularly for the ordinary seamen.

Now every detail of the *Golden Hinde*'s life and times can be explored; from her lower deck with its impressive armoury of cannon, the Poop Deck where Drake painted landscapes and his private cabin where he studied his navigational charts on a great oaken carved table chained to the floor. A legend, then and now; referred to as *El Draque*, The Dragon, by the Spanish. Here, bathed in the mellow light afforded by the latticed windows and among timbers permeated with the aromas of linseed and beeswax, you can see the replica of Drake's legendary drum and the crude cross-staff used by him to assess a rudimentary latitude; often known as Jacob's staff.

SHAKESPEARE'S GLOBE THEATRE

"Cram within this wooden O
The very casques that did affright the air at Agincourt..."

(Henry V, Act I Scene IV.)

As the Globe Theatre, authentically constructed of oak, plaster and thatch, lives and breathes again today, so the works of Shakespeare come to life even more eloquently when seen where they were originally performed. For the entertainment afforded by his tragedies and comedies were not only fashionable and affordable, they also seem to have been 'fun'. The Elizabethan Londoners certainly thought so, flocking in their thousands for the cheap daylight performances on the rather bawdy Bankside which was easily reachable by foot across London Bridge. Built in 1599 to hold 3000 people, the Globe soon became the richest and most successful playhouse on Bankside; it was the first to be financed by a playing company of actors, self-funded in a syndicate by its eight leading players. Shakespeare by then was already a prolific playwright as well as actor, but his greatest plays including *Hamlet, Othello, Macbeth* and *King Lear* were all written for the Globe and performed there for nearly half a century.

The present International Shakespeare Globe Centre honouring his acknowledged universality was the brainchild of the American actor and director, Sam Wanamaker. When visiting London in 1949, he was somewhat disconcerted to find that the only recognition of the original Globe was a grimy plaque on the wall of a local brewery. He went on to enlist the help of many, including embroiderers from New Zealand and metal workers from around the world, in order to achieve an authentic reconstruction. The South African-born Theo Crosby was, for twenty-five years, the architect of the project. The Globe we see today opened for its first full season in June 1997 with, appropriately, a performance of Henry V; sadly a few years after the deaths of both Wanamaker and Crosby.

The new Globe was the first thatched-roof building erected in London since the Great Fire of 1666. The fragmented foundations revealed at the original site were enough to allow scholars to predict its shape and dimensions; the angle of 162 degrees between the wall remains of two bays enabled the deduction that the original Globe had twenty sides. Some concessions in the construction of the present building were necessary. The white lime wash had to be augmented with goat's hair instead of the traditional cow's hair, the roofing thatch is composed of water reed from Norfolk as the Thames Valley no longer has reed beds, the stair towers are broader and there are now four exits. It is estimated that the 1,500 people the building is licensed to hold would be able to exit in under three minutes.

The design of the present stage was extensively researched. The set of four embroidered hangings took 10,000 hours to make. Shakespeare's plays were, and are, performed in the open air from May to September. The audience sit on traditional wooden benches in the galleries or stand in the yard below the stage, designed to slope like the original into a drain; flooding from the tidal Thames could be problem. The archives relate that in 1624 all sorts of people went to the Globe; the "old and young, rich and poor, master and servants, papists and puritans". The dazzling stage jutting halfway out into the yard with its brilliant drama feasted the minds of the audiences as they had never known. They indulged in eating, drinking, commenting and other unmentionable activities as they watched. Queen Elizabeth enjoyed entertainment and insisted that her Christmas celebrations should include plays, enabling actors to remain in work and well rehearsed.

Now there is a permanent Exhibition dedicated to Shakespeare and his craft and an Education Department which welcomes over 50,000 students every year. Two restaurants with compelling views of the river and many other modern facilities including an indoor theatre on site;

the Inigo Jones Theatre. A set of plans found in Oxford, as recently as 1969, were used as a guide to its construction with small handmade bricks and neo-classical pediment. The present Inigo Jones Theatre thus adheres as closely as possible to what is known about an Elizabethan indoor theatre; one was used at nearby Blackfriars by the Shakespearian actors during winter, four centuries ago, to perform works that a fellow playwright prophetically described as "not of an age, but for all time".

USEFUL ADDRESSES AND TELEPHONE NUMBERS

Greenwich Local History Library
Woodlands, 90 Mycenae Road, London SE 3.
Tel: 020 8858 4631

Greenwich Borough Museum
232 Plumstead High Street, London SE18.
Tel: 020 8855 3240

Greenwich Historical Society
The Music Centre, Blackheath High Street,
Vanbrugh Park, Blackheath, London SE 3.
Tel: 020 8858 4631

Lewisham Local Studies and Archives Centre
Lewisham Library, 199-201 Lewisham High Street, SE13 6LG.
Tel: 020 8297 0682 Fax: 020 8297 1169
e-mail: localstudies&Lewisham.gov.uk

Woolwich Town Hall (Borough Offices for Greenwich)
Wellington Street, London SE 18.
Tel: 020 8854 8888

Captain Cook Memorial Museum
Grape Lane, Whitby, North Yorkshire Y022 4BA
Tel/Fax: 01947 601900. www.cookmuseum.whitby.co.uk

Woolsthorpe Manor
23 Newton Way, Woolsthorpe by Colsterworth, near Grantham, Lincs
NG33 5NR (off A1) **Tel**: 01476 860 338
Open: w/e March and Oct. Wed-Sun April-Sept
Grantham Tourist Info. **Tel:/Fax**: 01476 406166

NOTABLE DATES

1st Century
0	Greenwich – Celtic *Conti* and *Atrebates* tribes
43-45	Romans build road from Dover to Thames at Greenwich

2nd Century
100-178   Claudius Ptolemy, astronomer and geographer, insists earth centre of universe; Refraction of Light experiments

3rd Century
270   Magnetic compass definitely known to be used in China

5th Century
430   Final Romans coins known at Greenwich
455-484   Saxon burial mounds in Greenwich Park area
Market established at *Grene Wic* (wic = market)

7th Century
685   Earliest vertical sundial in UK, at Bewcastle Cross, Cumbria

9th Century
870   Candles with lines at intervals used to tell time in England
871   King Alfred enthroned – disposes of Danes
Inherits Greenwich, Woolwich and Lewisham

11th Century
1000   Building of observatories revived in Asia
Magnifying glass known in Arabia
1012   Archbishop Alfege martyred at Greenwich by Vikings
1081   Greenwich confirmed as belonging to the Abbey of St Peter, Ghent, by William the Conqueror

1085	Greenwich and Woolwich appear as *Grenviz* and *Hulviz* in Domesday Book
1090	China develops very sophisticated water clock with earliest recorded 'escapement'

12th Century

1172	China publishes printed document describing the water clock with balance escapement
1180	Written evidence in *De Nominibus Utensilium* of compass used at sea by schoolmaster, prolific writer and scientist Alexander Neckham

13th Century

1268	Roger Bacon, scientific experimenter, notes magnifying glass used on the Continent

14th Century

1366	Edward III takes over Greenwich 'for security reasons'
1376	House of Friars established at Greenwich
1381	Peasants' Revolt ends on Blackheath

15th Century

1413-22	Henry V confiscates monastery and creates Manor of Greenwich
1433	Humphrey, Duke of Gloucester, encloses Greenwich Park, builds tower and house, Bellacourt, where friars lived
1447	Duke Humphrey dies under arrest; estate passes to Margaret of Anjou, wife of Henry VI
1482	Birth of Peter Henlein in Nuremberg; develops mainspring and pioneers 'the watch'
1485-1509	Henry VII rebuilds Bellacourt at Greenwich as Palace of Pleasaunce (Placentia)
1491	Henry VIII born at Placentia

16th Century

1509-47	Henry VIII succeeds. Marries Catherine of Aragon in the Chapel of Observant Friars at Placentia Greenwich now principal royal palace
1511	Greenwich Armoury started
1512-13	Henry VIII founds Woolwich and Deptford Dockyards
1515	Greenwich watchtower rebuilt as hunting lodge Tournament facilities built on site of NMM
1516	Mary Tudor born at Placentia
1540	Henry VIII installs Astronomical Clock at Hampton Court
1543	Nicholas Copernicus publishes epic work declaring a sun-centred solar system just before his death
1547-58	Deaths of Henry VIII, Edward VI and Mary Tudor
1558	Elizabeth I succeeds
1577	Francis Drake begins round-the-world voyage from Greenwich
1583	Drum water clock now in use

17th Century

1603	Death of Elizabeth I
1603-25	James I of England (VI of Scotland)
1608	Telescope marketed by Hans Lippershey
1609	Galileo develops the first astronomical refracting telescope
1613	James I gives Greenwich to his wife, Anne of Denmark
1616	Inigo Jones begins Queen's House (until 1619)
1624	Submarine demonstrated in Thames Estuary to James I by Cornelis Drebbel of Holland
1625	Charles I succeeds
1629-35	Queen's House completed for Queen Henrietta Maria
1660	Robert Hooke develops hairspring for watches
1662	Charles II gives his patronage to the 'Group of Thinkers' of 1645 and the Royal Society comes into being New Greenwich Palace begun by John Webb

	Queen's House partly remodelled and park redesigned
1666	Isaac Newton works out the mathematics needed to determine the mass of the earth for Laws on Gravitation
1668	First reflecting telescope by Isaac Newton
1671	Anchor escapement now used in pocket watches
1672	Royal Observatory Greenwich commissioned
1675	First Royal Astronomer, John Flamsteed, until 1719 Christian Huygens develops balance spring for watch; more functional and can be concealed in pocket
1676	John Tompion installs now-famous clocks in Octagon Room, Flamsteed House
1677	Simple Microscope with single lens invented by Antoni van Leeuwenhoek of Holland
1680	Christopher Wren becomes President of the Royal Society Royal Hospital for Soldiers founded in Chelsea
1685	Theory of Gravity (earth exerts constant force on falling bodies) expounded by Isaac Newton
1688-1702	Joint reign of William III and Mary II of Holland Queen's House becomes official residence of the Ranger of Greenwich Park
1689	Isaac Newton calculates speed of sound
1692	Death of Mary II just after reviving idea of using unfinished Greenwich Palace site as hospital for seamen
1696	Foundation stone laid for Royal Naval Hospital at Greenwich by Christopher Wren and John Evelyn

18th Century

1702	Queen Anne begins reign (until 1715)
1705	First 42 Pensioners arrive at Greenwich Hospital
1708	James Thornhill starts painting Dining Hall, Greenwich
1712	John Flamsteed furiously burns 300 copies of his pirated observations at the Royal Observatory St Alfege's Church collapses (rebuilt 1714 by Nicholas

	Hawksmoor – tower 1730 by John James)
1714	George I arrives at Greenwich – Hanover Dynasty begins Board of Longitude set up – offers prizes to anyone able to determine longitude at sea
1718	Edmond Halley predicts return of his comet Sir John Vanbrugh begins Vanbrugh Castle, Greenwich
1719	Mrs Flamsteed strips the Royal Observatory after husband's death, including John Tompion's clocks from Octagon Room
1720	2nd Royal Astronomer, Edmond Halley, until 1742
1725	Mrs Flamsteed officially publishes results of husband's observations
1727	George II succeeds – Queen Caroline lives in Queen's House
1730	Clockmaker John Harrison journeys to London and calls at the Royal Observatory – referred to George Graham
1742	3rd Royal Astronomer, James Bradley, until 1762
1752	Captain Cook starts three-year stint on colliers off East Coast
1755	James Cook joins Royal Navy as Able Seamen
1758	Return of Halley's Comet Greenwich Hospital School (Charity Boys since 1715)
1759	John Harrison completes H4
1760	George III begins reign
1762	4th Royal Astronomer, Nathaniel Bliss, until 1764
1765	5th Royal Astronomer, Nevil Maskelyne, until 1811
1766	The *Nautical Almanac* published
1772	Captain Cook sails on *Resolution* with watch K1 on trial
1773	Longitude Board finally pays John Harrison prize money
1779	Interior of Royal Naval Hospital Chapel at Greenwich burns out (rebuilt 1789) Louis Recordon, London, takes out patent for self-winding pocket watch
1781	Uranus discovered by William Herschel
1791	Ordnance Survey Mapping begun using the Bradley Meridian at the ROG

19th Century

1800	Alessandro Volta designs electric battery – Voltaic cell
1803	John Dalton expounds atomic theory
1810	Carriage clocks made by Breguet firm in France
1811	6th Royal Astronomer, John Pond, until 1835
1815	Ranger of Greenwich Park goes to live in Chesterfield House on Croom Hill (now Ranger's House Museum)
1820	George IV reigns until 1830
1821	André Ampère formulates Laws of Electrodynamics
	Hans Oersted notes electromagnetic rotation with compass needle and electric current
1823	Death of Sir John Angerstein, resident of Greenwich and leading founder member of Lloyds Marine Insurance. The following year the National Gallery formed using 38 of his paintings acquired for the nation; displayed at his former home in Pall Mall until the present building in Trafalgar Square was constructed (1832-38).
1828	Caroline Herschel awarded Gold Medal of the Royal Astronomical Society
1830	William IV reigns until 1837
1831	British Association for Advancement of Science founded
	Michael Faraday discovers electromagnetic induction
1833	Time Ball installed at Royal Observatory Greenwich
1835	7th Royal Astronomer, Sir George Biddell Airy, until 1881
	Charles Babbage designs mechanical computer
1837	Queen Victoria reigns until 1901
	Samuel Morse begins to develop code system of 'dots and dashes' for telegraphic communication
1840	Electric clocks on market – with batteries in pendulum bob
1851	Great Exhibition in Hyde Park
	George Biddell Airy installs new Transit Circle, ROG
	Longitude 0° established at Greenwich

	Jean Foucoult invents pendulum that demonstrates rotation of earth on axis, then gyroscope
1852	Greenwich Mean Time sent out from Royal Observatory for first time by electric telegraph
1859	Big Ben installed at Westminster – clock invented by E B Denison (later Lord Grimthorpe)
1865-6	The *Great Eastern* lays first successful transatlantic submarine cable made at Greenwich, with help of GMT telegraphed for exact calculation of longitude
1869	Royal Naval Hospital closes at Greenwich
1873	Royal Naval College transfers from Dartmouth to Greenwich Present site of Neptune Hall built on as gymnasium
1876	Alexander Graham Bell invents telephone
1877	Thomas Edison invents phonograph (first gramophone) and electric light bulb (1879) plus 1300 other items
1880	GMT – legal time of UK (British Standard Time)
1881	8th Royal Astronomer, Sir William Christie, until 1910
1884	Longitude 0° at Greenwich – declared Prime Meridian of the World and official basis of International Time Zone System
1885	The Great Wheel built at Greenwich for Earl's Court Exhibition
1894	28-inch Great Equatorial Telescope installed at ROG Work begins on South Building ROG

20th Century

1900	Max Planck establishes quantum theory
1901	Queen Victoria dies and Edward VII succeeds (until 1910) First British submarine, Holland I, launched by Vickers; named after US inventor
1902	Greenwich Foot Tunnel opened
1905	Einstein publishes Theory of Relativity
1910	9th Royal Astronomer, Sir Frank Dyson

1910	French first broadcast time
	George V begins reign (until 1936)
1914	Wrist watches made available to service personnel and found invaluable
1916	Einstein publishes more on Theory of Relativity
1919	Expedition to Principe, W Africa, to observe solar eclipse led by Arthur Eddington, Professor of Astronomy at Cambridge, proved Einstein's theory that light from distant stars is bent by gravity of sun
1921	Einstein awarded Nobel Peace Prize
1923	First broadcast of Big Ben striking the hour
1924	BBC first broadcast Greenwich Time Signal
	A National Naval and Merchant Service Museum is proposed at Greenwich
	John Harwood patents self-winding wristwatch
1926	John Logie Baird demonstrates black and white television (colour in 1928)
1927	New York to London radiotelephone service begun
1928	British Association for Advancement of Science granted Royal Charter
1930	Edwin Hubble confirms expanding universe
1931-32	John Cockroft and Ernest Walton develop first particle accelerator to 'split up' atomic nucleus of lithium
1933	10th Royal Astronomer, Sir Harold Spencer Jones, until 1955
1934	National Maritime Museum founded
1935	Alan Turing, aged 23, publishes paper describing hypothetical computer machine mechanising word functions
1936	Edward VIII reigns and abdicates
	George VI succeeds (until 1952)
1937	National Maritime Museum opened by King George VI as the first official engagement of reign
1939	Painted Hall in Royal Naval College, Greenwich, restored; used as officers' mess during war

1945	Decision to move remaining functions of Royal Observatory to Herstmonceux in Sussex
1948	200-inch (508 cm) Hale reflector telescope at Mount Palomar, USA
1950	Electromagnetic watches powered by tiny batteries
1952	Queen Elizabeth II begins reign
1954	The *Cutty Sark* moves into dry dock at Greenwich
1955	Atomic Clocks in use
	Atoms for Peace Conference organised by Neils Bohr
1956	11th Royal Astronomer, Sir Richard Woolley, until 1971
1960	Flamsteed House, ROG, opened to public
1961	First Man in Space, Yuri Gagarin
1967	Royal Observatory Greenwich becomes part of NMM
1968	Refurbishment of National Maritime Museum
1969	July 20 *Apollo* 11 lands – first men on the moon
1970	John Harrison's cottage at Barrow-on-Humber demolished while awaiting preservation order
1972	12th Royal Astronomer, Sir Martin Ryle, until 1982
1976	236-inch (599 cm) reflector telescope in USSR
1978	Personal computers on market
1979	UK infrared telescope (UKIRT) established on Hawaii
1982	13th Royal Astronomer, Sir Francis Graham Smith, until 1990
1984	Newton Telescope transferred to Canary Islands from Royal Observatory site at Herstmonceux
1986	GMT succeeded by UTC (Co-ordinated Universal Time based on International Atomic Time)
	Restoration begins on Queen's House, Greenwich
1990	Hubble Space Telescope launched
	Royal Observatory moves from Herstmonceux to Cambridge
1991	14th Royal Astronomer, Arnold Wolfendale, until 1995
1992	Major restoration begins of Royal Observatory
1995	15th Royal Astronomer, Sir Martin Rees

1996	Replica of Shakespeare's Globe Theatre opens on Bankside
1997	Royal Naval College, Greenwich, closes
	Neptune Hall, NMM, demolished for redevelopment
	The Greenwich Foundation formed
	Greenwich becomes World Heritage Site
1998	Royal Observatory closes in Cambridge – some functions return to Greenwich
1999	New Neptune Court, NMM, opened by the Queen
	31 December – Millennium Concert, Greenwich, linked by satellite and terrestrial TV worldwide

BIBLIOGRAPHY & FURTHER READING

The Maritime Yearbook(s) – Annual Magazine(s) of the Friends of the National Maritime Museum
Maritime Greenwich – The World Heritage Site, Official Guide
Kristen Lippincott, *A Guide to the Old Royal Observatory*
Jonathan Betts, Curator of Horology, NMM, *Harrison*
R J & C Godley, *Historic Greenwich – Millenium 2000*
Clive Aslet, *The Greenwich Millenium*
Charles Jennings, *Greenwich – The Place Where Days Begin and End*
E R Turner, *The Reverend John Flamsteed, 1646-1719, The First Astronomer Royal and Rector of Burstow*
Smallfield and Burstow Parish News
Mark Fryar, *Some Chapters in the History of Denby (John Flamsteed Ch IX)*
WEA, Barrow upon Humber, *John Harrison's Village*
H Gray and Neil Wilkyn, *The Manor of Barrow*
J W P Cherry (Churchwarden), *Barrow – A Short Guide*
Trevor I Williams, *Our Scientific Heritage*
Encyclopaedia Britannica
Oxford Dictionary of Quotations
Geoffrey Tweedale, *Calculating Machines and Computers*
Christopher St. J. H. Daniel, *Sundials*

Every effort has been made to contact copyright holders and we apologise for any unintentional errors or omissions.

Cover Design:	The Digital Canvas Company Forres Scotland bookcovers@digican.co.uk
Layout:	Stephen M.L. Young stephenmlyoung@aol.com
Font:	Adobe Garamond (11pt)

Copies of this book can be ordered via the Internet:

www.librario.com

or from:

Librario Publishing Ltd
Brough House
Milton Brodie
Kinloss
Moray IV36 2UA
Tel /Fax No 01343 850 617